Canoeing the California Highlands

A Quiet Water Guide To Paddler's Paradise

John Coale

Changing Sky Publications ~ Cedar Ridge, CA

Readers should pay strict attention to the advisory
statements of each listing in this book and
should consult current information sources to obtain
up-to-date conditions at any of these places.

Although the author and publisher have exhaustively
researched all sources to ensure the accuracy and
completeness of the information contained in this
book, we assume no responsibility for errors, inaccu-
racies, omissions or any other inconsistency herein.
Any slights against people or organizaitons are unin-
tentional.

ISBN: 0-9662821-0-8
Library of Congress Catalog Card Number: 98-96050

First Edition Printed 1998
Printed in the United States of America

Produced by Changing Sky Publications
P.O.Box 1390
Cedar Ridge, CA 95924

Acknowledgements

The author would like to express his heartfelt thanks to the following people and organizations for their help and support: **Len Gorsky** for being my computer guru and for taking me to Yosemite so I could remember the world of nature, **Joyce Wilson** for being my best paddling companion and for unending moral support, **Chalk Bluff Inc** for their beautiful digital relief map, which is the basis for the back cover of this book, the **US Geographical Survey** and the **US Forest Service** for making some great maps, **Gary Johnson** for getting me out on the Big River-**Taiowa Coale** for being a sweet child and great paddling companion, **Linda Haldane** of Haldane Computers for aiding me in my times of computer need, **Jim Woodward** of **California Parks & Recreation** for his aerial photography and **Sue Flynn** for proofreading and editing.

Preface

This book came from my desire to get on the water in a canoe. When I started this book I had just begun my adventures as a paddler. I had only been to three or four of the places listed here. I sought out all the resources I could get my hands on: campground guides, Geographical Survey maps, Forest Service maps, kayaking and fishing guidebooks; whatever had to do with water in northern California. In my search for places to go canoeing I found that there was no book available that could tell me where to go.

As I got more and more into my search for the coolest places to paddle, I discovered that I actually lived in one of the best paddling areas of the world. I compiled a list of over 180 places to go canoeing. When I finally ceased my frenzied search for "canoeable water" and looked at the notes I had scrawled, I realized I had the makings of a great resource book for anyone who wished to do quiet water paddling in northern California.

Contents

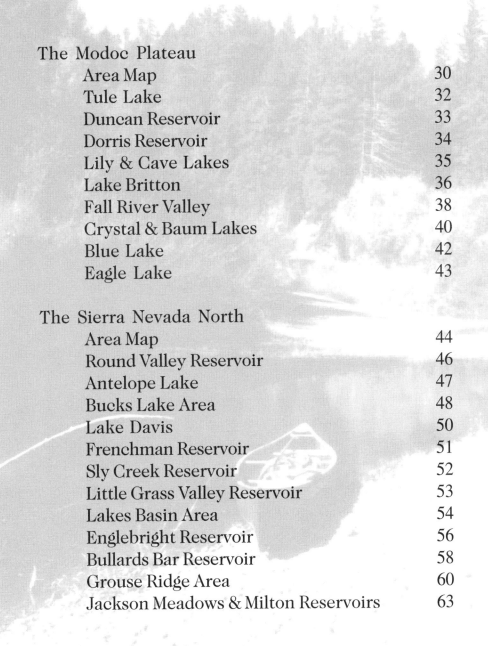

The Tahoe Sierra

Introduction

Paddler's Paradise

I have the great good fortune to live in California my whole life. It has been an even greater privilege to canoe the beautiful waters of the California highlands. These mountains of California are truly a paddler's paradise.

All these bodies of water would be considered quiet water and are appropriate for all levels of paddling skill. Some of these locations have incredible natural beauty, others offer the adventure of paddle-in camping across a lake or an opportunity for long distance paddling. Still others provide the paddler with complete quiet and solitude on small lakes with no power boats or jet skis.

Every canoeist dreams of living the life of Longfellow's *Hiawatha*. We sometimes need a guide to give us some knowledgeable, friendly advice. *Canoeing the California Highlands: A Quiet Water Guide to Paddler's Paradise* is that guide. You will be led to a wonder filled experience of paddling the exquisitely beautiful quiet water of the California mountains.

My criteria for deciding which lakes to put into this book was simple. First, a lake had to be accessible by two wheel drive vehicle, granted some of the road are a little rough, but passable. I excluded lakes whose access roads required four wheel drive. Second, the lake itself had to be condusive to quiet water paddling and have a minimum level of natural beauty. I excluded some lakes that were too small and most of the large reservoirs: Shasta, Folsom, Don Pedro, etc. The really big reservoirs tend to be overrun with people in power boats and jet skis and the water levels get drawn down so much that they get a really ugly case of reservoir ring.

Whether your pleasure is investigating the coves of a lake shoreline, navigating the twists and turns of a lake-filled river canyon or floating quietly in the middle of a serene high mountain lake, you will find your paddler's paradise within the pages of this book. This is your invitation to take part in an adventure of exploration and discovery.

> "...O'er the water floating, flying
> Through the shining mist of morning
> 'Til the birch canoes seemed lifted
> High into the seas of splendor..."
>
> Song of Hiawatha, Longfellow

Mount Lassen towers over Manzanita Lake

Mystery Lake?

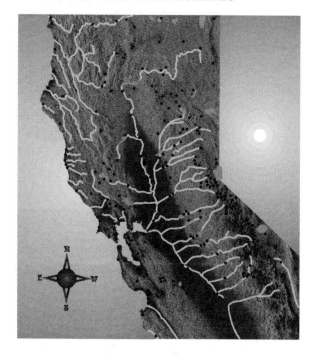

Map Legend

Using This Book

Using this book is easy. Read it, find a body of water on which you wish to paddle, and go there. Although the listings in this book will give you a thorough image of what you can expect of a place, there is nothing like being there and doing your own explorations.

Maps

There is a map for each listing which will give you an idea of the shape and proportions of any given location and the surrounding vicinity. The map legend at left has the symbols you need to find your way around on the maps. Every attempt has been made to make the maps as accurate as possible using the most up-to-date resources available. The maps are not meant to be exact. They will give a good idea of where things are located. However, there may be some small discrepancies, and an updated brochure or map from a local information source is your best bet for exact locations. See the *Resources* section of each listing.

Pictures

I have included in every listing photographs of the location in order to give you a visual reference. However, the true beauty of a place can never be known until you see it for yourself.

Description

This section gives you a basic idea of the setting - elevation, size of the water body, potential wildlife sightings and any special features you might like to check out.

Camping

This section tells you where in the area you can pitch your tent and cook your meals. It tells you what conveniences and amenities are available, whether or not you need to pay a fee and whether or not you can make reservations. Campgrounds run the gambit between a semi-flat place to pitch a tent with a fire-ring to full amenities with flush toilets and hot showers. Campground reservations can be made through the California Campground Reservation System. There is a service charge on top of the campground fee. They can be reached at: 800-444-7275.

Many areas have vacation cabin rentals that are available by the day or the week. These can be a nice alternative to camping out, especially during inclement weather. A list of available rentals can usually be obtained from the local Chamber of Commerce.

Directions

It's hard to get someplace if you don't have directions. Obviously, this section will tell you how to get there.

Resources   This section will tell you what maps are available for the area listed. They include National Forest maps from the U.S. Forest Service (USFS), which cover large areas and topo maps from the U.S. Geological Survey (USGS), that show the details of the topography.

Two of the best all around map resources are DeLorme's *Northern California Atlas & Gazetteer* and *Southern California Atlas & Gazetteer*. These books contain topo maps for all of California and cover all of the locations listed in *Canoeing The California Highlands*.

The most updated maps tend to be the U.S. Forest Service maps of national forests. They are very accurate and fairly inexpensive. You should also get a good map or atlas of California roadways. The American Automobile Association and Rand McNally both make good road maps.

Most of these resources can be obtained at your local outdoor recreation or book store. See *Suggested Reading: Maps*, page 117, for USFS and USGS ordering information.

Advisory   This section serves to warn you of any dangers or problems you might encounter including regular windy conditions, bears, power boat traffic, availability of drinking water, and anything else that might prove to be a problem if you are unprepared.

Information   This section will give you someone to contact about the availability of campsites, water levels, current weather & road conditions, etc. They will often have a brochure or map available.

Artist: F.L. Jaques   Courtesy Minnesota Historical Society

The canoe is light, swift, safe, graceful and easily moved.

Who, among the hard workers of our cities, need two months vacation, and can only get away from the desk or office for two weeks?

Who feels the confined work tell on his lungs, or his eyes, or shudders at the tremulousness of the shoulders and arms which precedes the breaking down from overwork?

All this can be cured by the sun and the wind and the delicious splash of the river on face and breast and arms. Those are they to whom a canoe is a godsend. They can get more health and strength and memorable joy out of a two-weeks' canoe trip than from a lazy, expensive and seasick voyage to Europe, or three months dawdle at a fashionable watering place...canoes are for pleasure...canoes are natural!

From "Canoeing On The Connecticut"
by John Boyle O'Reilly (1844-1890)

Shooting the Rapids, Francis Ann Hopkins, 1879
National Archives of Canada, C-002774

The First Lucky Journey

My first canoeing trip as an adult was with my nine year old daughter and my best friend's fifteen year old son. We set off across Lake Tahoe for Emerald Bay in an overloaded canoe with only two life jackets. Between the afternoon winds and the power boats, we were paddling through 2-3 foot waves coming from every direction. After three and a half miles of terror-ridden paddling, we entered Emerald Bay and were almost thrown out of the boat by a 4 foot wake from the "Tahoe Queen" paddle wheeler. The next day we paddled back to the car at 7:00 in the morning. The water was pure flat glass and I felt like Hiawatha. We had a great time, but we were very lucky not to capsize in the frigid waters of Lake Tahoe. I'd rather be skilled than lucky.

The Author

Canoeing Safety

Proper Training

When canoeing there are two basic skills that you must know, how to canoe and how to swim. In many areas groups like the Red Cross offer instruction in swimming and certified canoeing classes. Classes are available for beginning canoeing, intermediate river canoeing and advanced whitewater paddling. Call your local Red Cross for classes in your area. Many canoe and kayak stores also offer instruction on canoeing and kayaking skills. It also pays to thoroughly read a good basic canoeing book that covers types of canoes, paddle strokes, canoe equipment and other useful information specific to paddle sports.

Personal Flotation Devices

A personal flotation device (PFD) is what we all used to call a life preserver. It keeps you afloat when you're in the water. The only kind worth wearing is a vest style, Coast Guard approved, Type III PFD. The horse collar style life preservers should be avoided. They tend to scratch your neck and don't really supply adequate flotation. The law says you should wear a PFD at all times when you're on the water. You should always have a PFD available. Young children, whitewater paddlers, and poor swimmers should always wear a PFD whenever they are on or near the water, no exceptions.

Power Boat Wakes

One of the most potentially dangerous hazards of canoeing is power boats. You will find them on almost every reservoir or lake that allows them, particularly in the summer months. They are usually, but not always, driven by polite, considerate, sober people. They might not see you and can run you down or tip you over with their wakes. Occasionally, a power boater will see you in your canoe and will slow down to avoid "waking you up." But often they will pass by you at speeds of up to 50 m.p.h. and send a series of 2-3 foot wakes careening toward your not-so-stable canoe. The best way to handle power boats is to stay out of their way. When there are lots of power boats about, stay near the shoreline. Power boats tend to stay in deeper water when they are running at high speeds. When a big wake bears down on you, try to avoid taking it broadside. If you turn into the wake at about a 45 degree angle, it will lessen the side to side rocking effect. If you are paddling into or out of a campsite on a lake or reservoir, leave early in the morning, when the water is calm, before the wind comes up and the power boats get out on the water.

Natural Disasters

One of the main reasons we canoe is so we can get out into nature. The beauty and grandeur inspire a sense of awe and wonder. There are those times, however, when we must realize that we are not only a part of nature, but a very small part. The natural world is way bigger than we are. Nature will most often heal us, but it can hurt us and even kill us.

Wind-blown or boat-wake waves and strong river currents can take away your control of the canoe and dump you right in the water. Once you are in the water you are subject to the dangers of hypothermia and drowning. Drowning is where you breathe water instead of air, a practice best left to fish. Hypothermia is where your body temperature drops way below normal. You can slip into a coma and die if you don't deal with it correctly and immediately. You can get hypothermia when you get wet. Water as warm as 55 degrees can suck the heat out of your body in a very short time. In very cold water, you can lose control of your limbs in as little as 5 minutes. Except in summer, at lower elevations, the water in northern California is always 55 degrees or colder. If you get dunked in cold water, get out and get warm and dry as quickly as possible. For proper treatment of hypothermia see a first aid book or, better yet, take a first aid training class. With proper training and equipment, a warm fire, and a dry set of clothes, these dangers can be easily avoided.

Storms, Lightning & Blustery Winds

Storms are the primordial force that created our watery world. Without them there would be no water and no canoeing. Rain itself is pretty much harmless to paddlers. In fact, canoeing in a warm, gentle spring rain can be a very pleasant experience (bring a rain coat or a set of dry clothes, remember hypothermia). Some of the other elements of a storm, are not so benign. Lightning can kill you and at the very least, scramble your brain. If a storm comes in and threatens lightning, get off the water immediately! Don't try to get back to the put-in, just get off the water until the storm is gone. Walk back along the shore if you have to and get your canoe later. As an object floating above the surface of the water on a lake you become a prime target for a lightning strike.

Another storm force to be reckoned with is strong winds. Most days in the mountains there will be some wind, particularly in the afternoons. Wind can also raise considerable waves on waters that are openly exposed. In heavy winds stay near shore and make your way back to the put-in.

A weather radio will keep you updated on the current storm conditions with forecasts of thunderstorms and winds to come.

Canoes in a Fog, Lake Superior, Francis Ann Hopkins
Glenbow Collection, Calgary, Canada

— —
————
— — *The Abysmal (Water)*
— —
————
— —

The Abysmal repeated.

> *If you are sincere,*
> *you have success in you heart,*
> *And whatever you do succeeds.*

Through repetition of danger we grow accustomed to it. Water sets the example for the right conduct under such circumstances. It flows on and on, and merely fills up all the places through which it flows; it does not shrink from any dangerous spot nor from any plunge, and nothing can make it lose its own essential nature. It remains true to itself under all conditions. Thus likewise, if one is sincere when confronted with difficulties, the heart can penetrate the meaning of the situation. And once we have gained mastery of a problem, it will come about naturally that the action we take will succeed. In danger all that counts is really carrying out all that has to be done ~ thoroughness ~ and going forward, in order not to perish through tarrying in danger.

> *I Ching*

It required some rudeness to disturb with our boat the mirrorlike surface of the water, in which every twig and blade of grass was so faithfully reflected; too faithfully indeed for art to imitate, for only Nature may exaggerated herself. The shallowest still water is unfathomable. Wherever the trees and skies are reflected, there is more than Atlantic depth.... We notice that it required a separate intention of the eye, a more free and abstracted vision, to see the reflected trees and the sky, than to see the lake bottom.

Henry David Thoreau

The Changing Seasons

California's weather is as diverse as its terrain. As the seasons change, so does the safety and accessibility of your canoeing experience. Rain and snow, wind and fog, heat and cold, all have their place and season. You have to be prepared for each one.

In springtime the weather can be very unpredictable, running the gambit between cold, windy rain to sunny and quite warm. Lakes are usually reaching their capacity and so are rivers. Full lakes are great, full rivers can be very dangerous. A river that is a class I or II in the late summer can be a class III to class VI (unrunnable) during spring run-off. Paddling on a full lake in warm weather beats an out-of-canoe swim in frigid, snow melt water on any given day. Around May or June the roads into the mountains start to open up. And then, there are those spring days when the wildflowers reach for the sun as it rises towards its apex, and the water lies glassy on a windless day - you'll swear you're in heaven and you'll never want to go back to work.

Summer brings intolerably hot temperatures to any place below 2000 feet elevation. Summer also brings the hoards of vacationers and power boaters out to the larger, more accessible reservoirs. The mountains are usually 10 to 20 degrees cooler than the lowlands. During the summer, if you want to paddle in solitude, you'll have to work for it, and drive the extra miles on the bumpier roads (or be really lucky).

Fall brings a break in the heat and often wetter, windier weather. It also brings out all those wonderful fall colors. Canoeing on a high mountain lake in early fall, among the aspen-covered shores is one of the great canoeing experiences. Fall in northern California can also bring on the delight of "Indian summer," when the temperature get into the '70s and the high clouds put on an art show of unparalleled beauty, and oohh the sunsets, "Red sky at night, canoer's delight."

As cold as winter can get, it can also be the best time of year to get away from the crowds. The water is too cold for water skiing or swimming and most campers don't want to brave the chilly nights. If you can take off when the rain and wind abate, you can often find a lake and campground all to yourself. Any place above 4,000 feet elevation tends to be closed or inaccessible because of snow, but there are plenty of low-lying lakes.

No matter what the season, if you get the urge to paddle, you can find the perfect place to go.

"Believe me, my young friend,
there is nothing
~absolutely nothing~
half so much worth doing
as simply messing about in boats."

River Rat, from "Wind In The Willows" by Kenneth Grahame

"You can never step in the same river twice."

Heraclitus

~

Be prepared to find canoeing a sometimes rough sport. There is plenty of hard work about it and a good deal of sunburn and blister...but if you have the true spirit of the canoeist, you will win for your pains an abundance of good air, good scenery, wholesome exercise, sound sleep, and something to tell about all your life.

Paraphrased from "Historic Water ways: Six Hundred Miles Of Canoe ing..." by Reuben Gold Thwaites (1853-1913)

~

The way of a canoe is the way of the wilderness and of freedom almost forgotten, the open door to waterways of ages past and a way of life of profound and abiding satisfaction.

Sigurd F. Olson, "The Lonely Land"

"Preparing for a trip is its own adventure."

Anonymous

~

"I only went out for a while and finally concluded to stay out till sundown, for going out, I found, was really going in."

John Muir, 1913

~

The real way to know water is not to glance at it here or there in the course of a hasty journey, nor to become acquainted with it after it has been partly civilized and spoiled by too close contact with the works of man. You must go to its native haunts; you must see it in youth and freedom; you must accommodate yourself to its pace, and give yourself to its influence, and follow its meanderings whithersoever they may lead you.

Henry Van Dyke (1852-1933)

What To Bring

Canoes

Canoes come in a variety of shapes, sizes and construction materials. What kind of canoe you get depends on what kind of canoeing you want to do. A canoe that holds a good straight line on a lake might not turn very well on a moving, winding river. A canoe that is great for casual day trips when all you have to carry are two people and a knapsack might not be big enough for paddle-in camping when you have to carry all your camping gear and food for a couple of days. A good book on basic canoeing will cover all the variables (see *Suggested Reading,* page 117, for a listing of canoeing books). If you plan on canoeing alone, check out what are called touring kayaks. All of the lakes in this book are perfect for touring and sea kayaks. The double bladed paddle can be much easier to work with when you're paddling alone. Canoe and kayak stores often have demonstration days where you can try out a variety of canoes and kayaks.

Paddles

The main criteria for a paddle is that it be the right size for you. Standing up with the tip of the paddle on the ground in front of you, the end of the handle should come to about your chin. This will allow you to paddle comfortably with the paddle at the right depth for efficient propulsion through the water. If you're a beginner, paddle design won't matter all that much at first, be it straight-shaft, bent-shaft, beaver tail, laminated, one piece, or whatever. You can save all that rigamarole for when you become a total canoeing fanatic (it takes about one month). Also, canoe demo days usually have a variety of paddles to try. If you are using a double-bladed kayak paddle, it should be from the ground to the tips of your fingers, reaching up and standing flat footed.

Clothing

Clothing is very important in canoeing. You want to be able to warm up or cool off. Several available layers are the way to go. If you think you might get wet, you should get into synthetics such as polypropylene underwear, pile sweaters and nylon windbreakers and pants. Wet cotton will drain your body heat away in a hurry, and will leave you vulnerable to hypothermia. Wool becomes heavy and cumbersome when it gets wet (it smells bad, too). Synthetics are lightweight, comfortable, warm when layered, and dry quickly when they get wet. Check you local outdoor recreation or paddlesport store. The nice thing about a retail store is that you get to see what you're buying before you buy it. You know it fits and you know if you like the color. Mail order paddling and camping supply companies have excellent prices on synthetic clothing.

Car Racks   Although canoeing the backwaters of your garage or yard can be a hoot, it's more fun if you actually take a canoe and put it on water; hence the necessity for canoe-carrying racks on your car or truck. You can get an inexpensive foam block and strap kit or you can spend hundreds of dollars for the multifaceted, super-yuppie, deluxe car racks that not only will carry your canoe, snow skis and bicycles, but it will also cook your food and guarantee nice weather.

If you're going to adventure out away from your canoe and you want it to be there when you get back, make sure you can lock it down. No, this is not being paranoid, canoes really do get stolen. A lock and chain through the car rack and the canoe thwart will do, as long as you have the kind of car rack that locks to your car.

Forgettable   I hate to sound like your mother, but don't forget your sunscreen. There are
Necessities   a few miscellaneous necessities that everyone needs and almost everyone forgets at one time or another - something to eat, drinking water or a good water filter, sunscreen, sunglasses, a hat, clothes to keep you warm and a change of clothes in case you get wet. All of these items should be in waterproof dry bags, specially made for this purpose, in case you capsize.

The old Lakota was wise. He knew that man's heart away from nature becomes hard; he knew that lack of respect for growing, living things soon led to lack of respect for humans too. So he kept his youth close to it's softening influence.

Chief Standing Bear, 1899

Whatever your paddling pleasure,
I hope this book helps guide you
to an enjoyable time on the water.

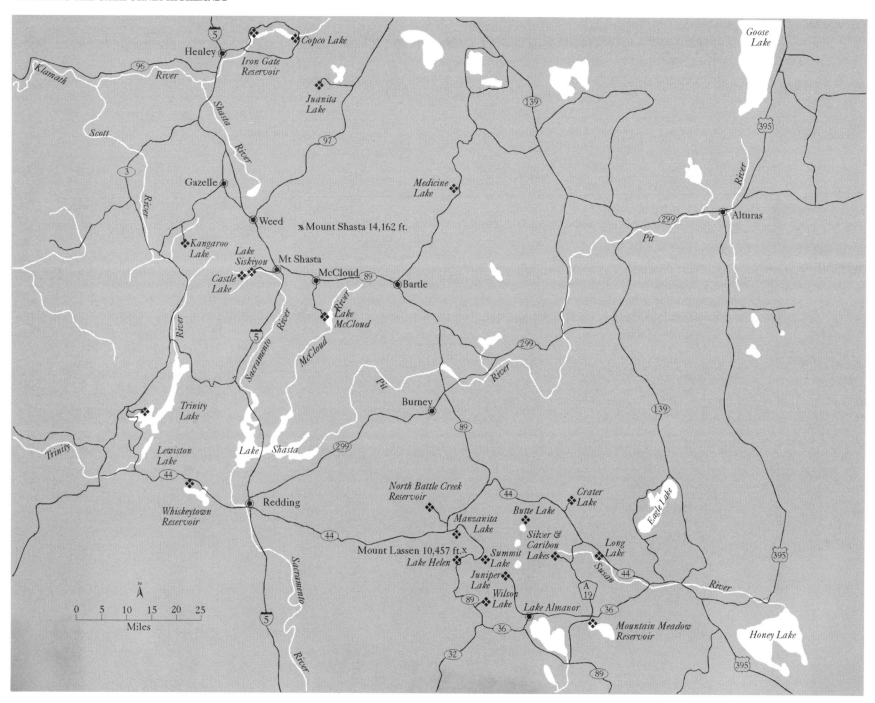

The Klamath/CascadeMountains

Basalt outcropping on Iron Gate Reservoir

The Klamath River flows into Copco Lake

Iron Gate Reservoir/Copco Lake

Description   Iron Gate Reservoir and Copco Lake offer a good opportunity to do some long distance paddling. Iron sits at 2,400 feet elevation and is about seven miles long. Copco Lake sits at 2,613 feet elevation and is about 5 miles long. At Copco's east end you can paddle up the Klamath River for quite a ways. In summer green algae grows in the water making swimming a disgusting prospect.

Camping   All these campgrounds have tables, firerings and toilets, no fee, no reservations: Mirror Cove, 10 sites, no water - Juniper Point, 9 sites, piped water - Camp Creek, 12 sites, piped water - Copco Cove, 1 site, no water - Mallard Cove, 1 site, no water. Bring your own water or a good water filter.

Directions   From Interstate 5 north of Yreka take the Henley/Hornbrook exit, go east on Copco Road for approximately 8 miles to campgrounds and boat ramps of Iron Gate Reservoir. For Copco Lake continue on Copco Lake Road past the Pacific Power plant. This road leads all the way around Copco Lake.

Resources   Iron Gate Reservoir/Copco Lake USGS topo maps, Klamath National Forest Map

Advisory   The wind really rips on these lakes and comes up without much warning.

Information   Pacific Power: 530-842-3521 and Copco Lake Store: 530-459-3655

Kangaroo Lake

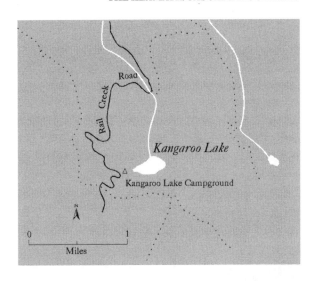

Description   This is one pretty little lake, perfect for just floatin' around. Although there is a small dam on Kangaroo Lake to deepen the water a bit, I would consider it a natural lake. It rests at 6000 feet elevation surrounded by granite, with 25 surface acres and is 100 feet deep at its deepest. Motors of any kind are prohibited, making this high mountain lake perfect for canoeing. You have to portage your canoe a short way in but it's worth it. There is a beach for swimming and a trail around the lake The Pacific Crest Trail is nearby for those who wish to attain the truly spectacular views of Kangaroo Lake and Scott Valley. Even the view from the picnic area in the parking lot is pretty spectacular.

Camping   Kangaroo Lake walk-in campground has 15 sites with tables, fireplaces, toilets and piped water for a fee; no reservations.

Directions   From Interstate 5 at Edgewood take the Old 99 Hwy north to Gazelle, go southeast on Gazelle/Callahan Road to Rail Creek Road, go southwest on Rail Creek Road to the lake and campground. The road in has some astoundingly beautiful views.

Resources   Scott Mountain topo map from the USGS; Klamath National Forest Map from the USFS, brochure from Scott River Ranger Station.

Advisory   Snow can make the lake inaccessible from late fall through early spring.

Information   Scott River Ranger District: 530-468-5351

Turquoise waters of Kangaroo Lake

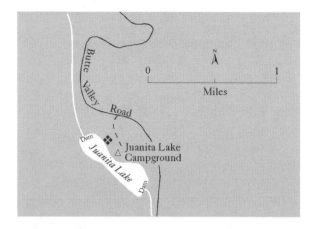

Juanita Lake

Description Juanita Lake lays in the shadow of an ancient volcano, Goosenest Mountain, at 5,100 feet elevation. Strangely, it has a dam at both ends of the lake. Motors are prohibited on Juanita Lake. One of the most pleasant floats I ever took was on Juanita Lake while the fiery colors of sunset reflected on the water. In the morning a delicate mist hovered just above the lake while the birds woke up and came to life. There is a 1.5 mile wheelchair accessible trail around the lake that make for a nice morning or evening stroll.

Camping Juanita Lake campground has 23 sites with tables, fireplaces, toilets and piped water for a fee, no reservations. The campground was very well maintained when I was there and is wheelchair accessible.

Directions From the town of Weed off Interstate 5 take Hwy 97 northeast for about 40 miles to the town of MacDoel, go west on Meiss Lake Road about 8.5 miles, go south on Butte Valley Road to the lake and campground.

Resources Klamath National Forest map, Panther Rock & MacDoel USGS maps.

Advisory "It's all right to have a good time."

Information Goosenest Ranger District: 530-398-4391

Ball Mountain rises behind Juanita Lake

Looking south across Juanita Lake

Medicine Lake

Description

This oval shaped, natural lake sits at 6,700 feet elevation atop ancient lava flows. Once you consider that Medicine Lake was formed when the center of a volcanic caldera filled with water, you get a whole new geological appreciation for this gorgeous natural lake. The water is a beautiful deep blue color. Unfortunately, this is an extremely popular lake in summer with lots of power boats, jet skis and noisy children in fluorescent colored bathing suits. However, if you get out on the water at sunrise, you can have the place almost all to yourself.

Nearby, tiny Blanche and Bullseye Lakes offer some float opportunities on very shallow waters. About 12 miles away are the geologic wonders of the Lava Beds National Monument with huge lava flows, ice caves, sink holes and a generally prehistoric feel.

Camping

All these campgrounds have tables, fireplace, toilets and piped water for a fee, no reservations: Headquarters, 10 sites - Medicine Lake, 22 sites - A.H.Houge, 24 sites - Hemlock, 24 sites. Bullseye Lake has a few primitive campsites with fireplaces but no tables, no toilets and no water for free, no reservations.

Directions

From Interstate 5 go east on Hwy 89 about 17 miles past the town of McCloud to the town of Bartle, shortly after Bartle go north on Forest Road 49 (sign says "Medicine Lake") for about 30 miles to the lake and campgrounds.

Resources

Modoc National Forest map, Medicine Lake USGS map.

Advisory

Due to afternoon winds, power boats and jet skis it is advisable to stay near shore. It can snow as late as May and as early as October. Closed in Winter.

Information

Modoc National Forest District Office: 530-667-2246

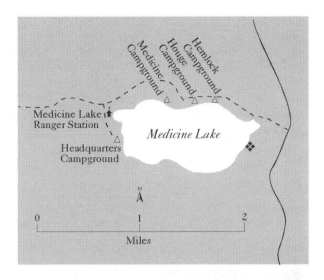

Medicine Lake

Bullseye Lake, more of a pond, really

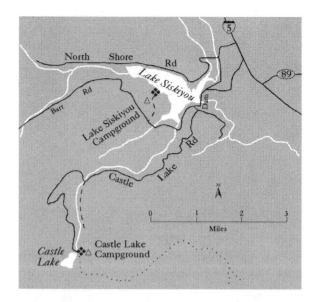

Lake Siskiyou & Castle Lake

Description Lake Siskiyou rests at about 3,100 feet elevation at the foot of Mount Shasta which hovers majestically on the northern horizon. There are 437 surface acres and more than 5 miles of shoreline to explore on this man-made reservoir. Boat speed is limited to 10 m.p.h. and there is a nice sandy swimming beach. This is a popular resort in the summer and with all the brightly colored swimsuits and beach umbrellas it usually looks more like a carnival than a mountain hideaway. When I was there they had a voyager-style canoe at the docks that looked like it seated 20 or more paddlers.

A few miles down the road and up the hill is Castle Lake. Castle Lake is a small, natural, alpine lake which sits in the shadow of Castle Crags in a glacial bowl filled with crystal clear snowmelt water at 5,400 feet elevation. There is a rock wall on one side of the lake and a gorgeous view of Mount Shasta to the northeast. There are some great day hikes in the area. No motors are allowed making this an idyllic mountain getaway for the paddler.

Camping Lake Siskiyou has 225 tent sites with running water, flush toilets, tables, fireplaces and showers for a fee; reserve through the Lake Siskiyou Camp Resort office, (see *Information, below*). Lodging units are also available.

Castle Lake campground has 6 sites for tents only about a half a mile from the lake with toilets, tables and fireplaces, but no water; no fees; no reservations.

Directions From Interstate 5 at Mount Shasta City go west on W.A.Barr to Lake Siskiyou. For Castle Lake continue on W.A.Barr past Lake Siskiyou, go left on Castle Lake Road to the lake and campground. On the way back down from Castle Lake you will get a spectacular view of Mount Shasta.

Resources Weed topo map from the USGS, Shasta/Trinity National Forest map from USFS.

Advisory Bring your own water. Snow can make the lake inaccessible from late fall through early spring. Midweek visits have better chances of getting a campsite.

Information Mount Shasta Ranger District, 530-926-4511; Lake Siskiyou Camp Resort, 530-926-2618

Mt. Shasta rises over Lake Siskiyou

Castle Lake

Lake McCloud

Description McCloud Lake is a gorgeous lake with emerald green water and narrow shores. It gets little, if any, use from power boat or jet skis. It rests among the pine trees of the Shasta National Forest at 3,000 feet elevation. The lake covers 520 acres and is perfect for a day's paddling exploration. The Pacific Crest Trail runs nearby through Ah-Di-Na campground.

Camping Ah-Di-Na campground has 16 sites with tables, fireplaces, piped water and flush toilets for a fee, no reservations. There is one undeveloped campground on the Star City Creek branch of the lake. You have to boat-in to the camp with no guarantee of much being there. Write and tell me if you find anything worthwhile.

Directions From Interstate 5 take Hwy 89 east to the town of McCloud, following the signs to "Lake McCloud" go south on Squaw Valley Road about 18 miles to the lake and campground.

Resources Shasta National Forest map, Lake McCloud USGS topo map.

Advisory Don't take life too seriously. It's not permanent. Occasionally it does snow here in the winter

Information McCloud Ranger District: 530-964-2184

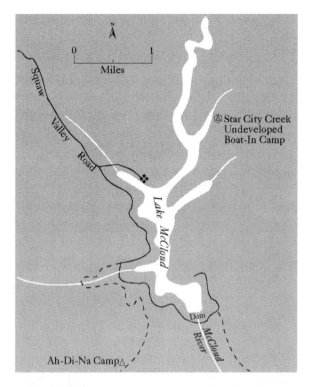

Lake McCloud

Still morning on Lewiston Lake

Lewiston Lake

The natural shoreline of Lewiston Lake is perfect for canoeing

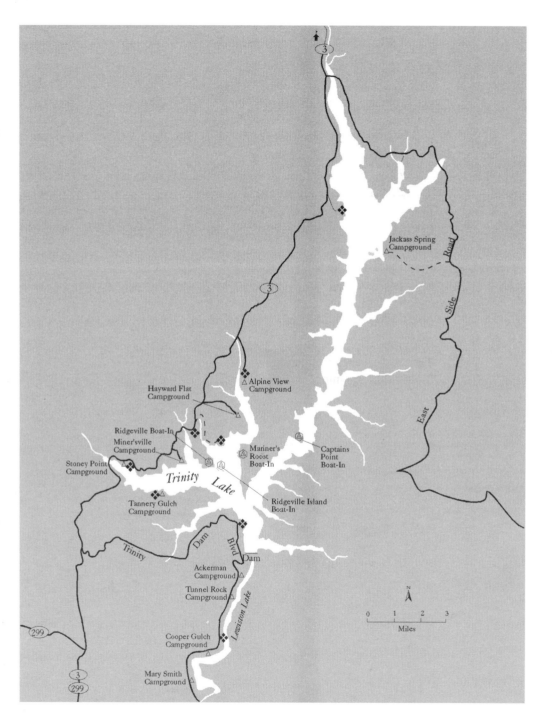

Lewiston & Trinity Lakes

Description Although Lewiston Lake is the afterbay for Trinity Lake, it is actually the better canoeing lake of the two. The lake has a very natural look because it is always full, giving shoreline water plants a chance to develop. It sits at 1,900 feet elevation, is 9 miles long and has a speed limit of 10 m.p.h. Idyllic paddling.

Trinity Lake sits at 2,300 feet near the granite peaks of the Trinity Alps. It is a large recreational lake with 17,000 surface acres and 145 miles of shoreline created by a dam on the Trinity River. There are hundreds of secluded, peaceful little coves to explore and great views of the Trinity Alps. Trinity Lake tends to be crowded with power boats and jet skiers. By mid summer, as the lake level lowers, it tends to get a bad case of reservoir ring. But, it does offer some long distance paddling and boat-in camping opportunities.

Camping There are four boat-in camps on Trinity Reservoir: Ridgeville, 21 sites - Ridgeville Island, 4 sites - Mariner Roost, 7 sites - Captains Point, 3 sites. All these camps provide toilets, fireplaces and tables but no water, no fees, no reservations.

There are 4 campgrounds along the west side of Lewiston Lake. Ackerman has 66 sites with running water, flush toilets, tables and fireplaces for a fee; no reservations. Mary Smith has 18 sites for tent only with running water, flush toilets, tables and fireplaces for a fee; no reservations. Cooper Gulch has 9 sites with vault toilets, tables and fireplaces but no water; no fee; no reservations. Tunnel Rock has 6 tent sites with vault toilets, tables and fireplaces but no water; no fee, no reservations.

Directions To get to Trinity Lake take Hwy 299 out of Redding west to Douglas City, take Hwy 299\3 north, where Hwy 299 splits off to go west to Eureka stay on Hwy 3 to the reservoir.

To get to Lewiston Lake go east on Trinity Dam Boulevard off Hwy 3 just southwest of Trinity Lake to Lewiston Lake and the campgrounds.

Resources Shasta/Trinity National Forest map from USFS, Trinity Dam, Papoose Creek, Covington Mill, Carville and Whiskey Hill Peak USGS topo maps.

Advisory Watch for power boats. Bring your own water or a water filter to the boat-in camps. Some campsites close or are hard to reach when water levels are low. Call ahead to the Ranger Station.

Information Weaverville Ranger Station: 530-623-2121

Trinity Lake

Ridgeville Island boat-in camp

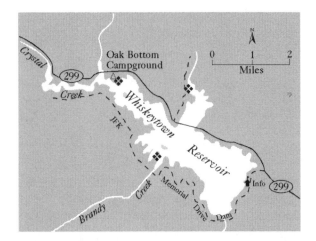

Whiskeytown Reservoir

Description   Whiskeytown Reservoir rests at 1,200 feet elevation just west of the town of Redding. The water is clear and the lake level is usually higher in the summer than in the winter (go figure). This is a good sized, man-made, recreational lake with 36 miles of shoreline and 3,220 surface acres. Due to it's easy accessibility, this reservoir tends to be inundated with people, power boats and jet skis in the summer. At the western end of Whiskeytown Reservoir where Crystal Creek enters the lake, the canoeing is very nice. The shallower water and narrower banks at the west end discourage fast boats and jet skis. There are some islands at this end of the lake to explore. Sailboats and windsurfers love Whiskeytown Reservoir for its consistent, strong winds, a condition that makes the middle of the lake somewhat hazardous for paddlers. There is some nice day hiking in the area including a couple of gorgeous waterfall: Brandy Creek Falls and Crystal Creek Falls.

Camping   Oak Bottom (101 walk-in sites) has tables, fireplaces, piped water, flush toilets and pay showers for a fee, reservations required in summer through Destinet at 800-365-CAMP.

Directions   From Interstate 5 at Redding take the Hwy 299 west exit and go west on Hwy 299 to the lake and campgrounds.

Resources   Shasta National Forest map from USFS, French Gulch, Whiskeytown and Igo topo maps from USGS.

Advisory   Watch out for power boats and jet skis. Winds tend to be strong and consistent. The middle of the lake can be quite harrowing for canoers.

Information   Whiskeytown National Recreation Area: 530-241-6584

Crystal Creek enters Whiskeytown Reservoir

Whiskeytown Reservoir from the information center

North Battle Creek Reservoir

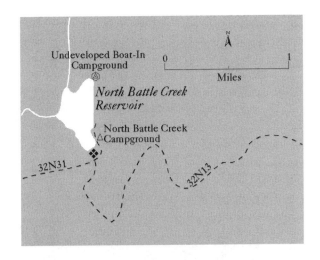

Description   North Battle Creek Reservoir is a small, isolated and often deserted reservoir. It is a good side trip to get away from the crowds when you're in the Mount Lassen area. This small natural looking lake is ideal for a lazy, pleasant paddle. The elevation at North Battle Creek Reservoir is 5,600. Gas motors are prohibited, so the air stays fume-free and the atmosphere is quiet and laid back.

Camping   There are 10 drive-to sites and 5 walk-in sites with tables, fireplaces, toilets and piped water for a fee, no reservations.

Directions   From Hwy 44 just east of the town of Viola and just west of the Hwy 44/89 junction is the sign for North Battle Creek Reservoir, take Forest Service Road 32N17 north for a little less than 4 miles, take Forest Service Road 32N31 west about 4 miles, then take Forest Service Road 32N18 about a half mile to the lake and campgrounds

Resources   Lassen National Forest map from USFS, Viola topo map from USGS.

Advisory   Late spring, winter and early fall snows can make the lake inaccessible.

Information   Pacific Gas & Electric: 530-386-5164

Small, isolated North Battle Creek Reservoir

Mount Lassen reflects in Manzanita Lake

Clear, blue Juniper Lake

Mountain meadow in Lassen National Park

Mount Lassen Area

Description   Mount Lassen is one of the truly awesome natural wonders of California. At 10,427 feet elevation it dominates the landscape here. This snow capped peak is the only active volcano in California and last erupted repeatedly from 1914-1921. The lakes at the base of this living behemoth provide a variety of canoeing experiences. Also, take the hike to the top of Mount Lassen. You won't regret it.

Butte Lake: man-made, stark, volcanic shoreline. Juniper Lake: good sized, pretty, forested shoreline, Mount Lassen in the distance. Manzanita Lake: idyllic, natural, beautiful, small, Mount Lassen looms large to the east reflecting in the water. Summit Lake: natural, small, shallow, pretty, high mountain. Lake Helen: very small, beautiful color blue, sits right below Mount Lassen's peak.

Camping   All these campgrounds lie within the boundaries of Lassen National Park which charges a $5/day fee in addition to any campground fees. The all have tables, fireplaces and toilets for a fee, no reservations: Juniper Lake, 18 sites for tent only, no water - Southwest, 21 walk in sites, piped water, flush toilets - Summit Lake South, 40 sites, piped water - Summit Lake North, 54 sites, piped water, flush toilets - Crags: 45 sites, piped water - Manzanita: 179 sites, piped water, flush toilets, showers - Butte Creek: 10 unimproved sites, no water - Butte Lake, a few sites, no water. Some campgrounds close early, call ahead.

Directions   For all lakes: from Interstate 5 in Redding take Hwy 36 east toward Lassen National Park. Juniper Lake: continue on Hwy 36 to the town of Chester, at Chester go north on Chester/Juniper Lake Road to the lake and campground (a long, rough road). Lake Helen: continue on Hwy 36 to the Hwy 36/89 junction, go north on Hwy 89 into Lassen National Park, the lake is on your left. Summit Lake: continue on Hwy 89, the lake is on your right. Manzanita Lake: continue on Hwy 89, the lake is on your left. Butte Lake: as you leave Lassen National Park go north on Hwy 89/44 to where Hwy 44 turns east, continue on Hwy 44 to the sign for Butte Lake, go south on Forest Service Road 32N21 to the lake and camp.

Resources   Lassen National Forest map from USFS - Manzanita Lake, West Prospect Peak, Prospect Peak, Lassen Peak, Reading Peak and Mount Harkness topo maps from USGS.

Advisory   Bring your own water or a water filter. Snow can make these lakes inaccessible in winter. Fishing is not allowed at Juniper Lake. Bring a Forest Service map.

Information   Lassen National Forest: 530-257-2151 or Lassen National Park: 530-595-4444

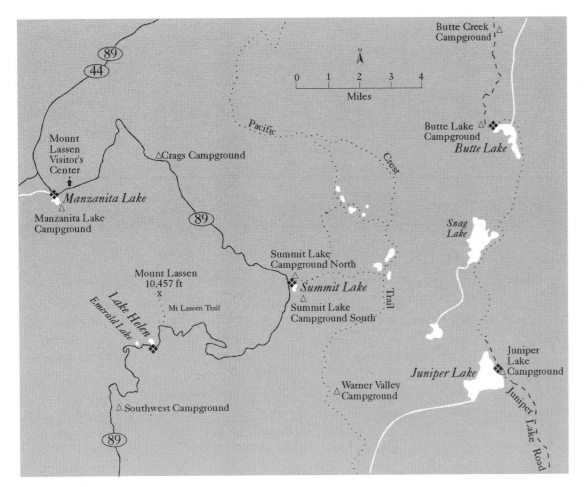

Mount Lassen rises above turquoise Lake Helen

Shallow, natural Summit Lake

Mount Lassen towers above everything

Butte Lake is surrounded by ancient lava flows

23

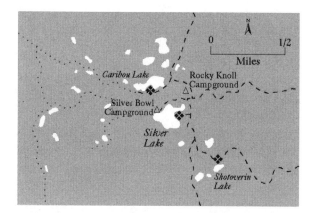

Silver & Caribou Lakes

Description   Silver Lake and Caribou Lake sit on the edge of the Caribou Wilderness at the headwaters of the Susan River. Both these lakes are natural lakes that have been augmented with small dams to give them some depth. Silver Lake is at 6,400 feet elevation and is a very pretty, small lake surrounded by well forested shores. Caribou Lake is at 6,500 feet elevation and is less forested. Caribou has the feeling of being higher up in the mountains even though it is only 100 feet higher.

This area is one of the premier hiking areas of California. The Caribou Wilderness has hundreds of miles of trails that pass by the many mountain lakes that dot the area. Whether in a canoe or on foot, this area is a nature explorer's dream come true.

Camping   Both these campgrounds have tables, fireplaces, toilets and piped water for a fee, no reservations: Rocky Knoll, 11 sites - Silver Bowl, 18 sites.

Directions   Silver Lake: From Hwy 36 east of Lake Almanor at the town of Westwood, take County Road A21 north about 12 miles to the sign for Silver Lake, take Silver Lake Road west to the lake and campground. Caribou Lake: stay on Silver Lake Road past Silver Lake to Caribou Lake.

Resources   Lassen National Forest map from USFS - Bogard Butte and Red Cinder topo maps from USGS

Advisory   Bring your own water or a water filter. Snow makes these lakes inaccessible in winter. Bring a Forest Service map.

Information   Lassen National Forest: 530-257-2151

Silver Lake

Caribou Lake

Crater Lake

Description Crater Lake is a gorgeous small lake where turquoise blue water fills an old volcanic caldera. There are no inlets or outlets, only the rain feeds Crater Lake. The lake rests at 6,800 feet with a surface area of 27 acres. Motors of any kind are prohibited, so paddlers can lay back and have a relaxing float. If you hike to the top of the lava flow that surrounds the lake you get a great view of this dead volcano. It is a powerful image to remember what this must have been like when this volcano was active.

Camping Crater Lake campground has 17 sites with table, fireplaces, vault toilets and available well water for a fee; no reservations.

Directions From Interstate 5 in Redding take Hwy 36 east toward Lassen National Park, continue on Hwy 36 past the town of Chester and Lake Almanor to the town of Westwood, from Westwood go north on County Road A21 to the junction with Hwy 44, go north on Hwy 44 to the Crater Lake turn off (Forest Service Road 32N08), take Crater Lake Road/32N08 about 7 miles to the lake and campground. The dirt road into Crater Lake is rough.

Resources Lassen National Forest map from USFS; Harvey Mountain and Pine Creek Valley topo maps from USGS.

Advisory The road in is rough. Snows make the lake inaccessible in winter

Information Lassen National Forest, 530-257-2151

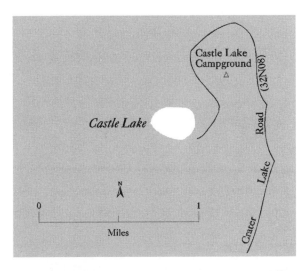

Aerial Photo of Crater Lake   *Courtesy of US Forest Service*

Crater Lake

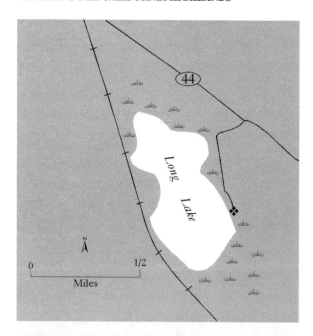

Long Lake

Description   Long Lake is a natural lake that sits at about 5,500 feet elevation. Actually, it's more of a marsh than a lake, but the water is deep enough to paddle and the lake big enough to get in some good strokes. There are no facilities at long lake. It is mostly used by fishermen in aluminum boats with electric motors. Freshwater marsh grasses cover much of the lake which is about a quarter mile wide and half mile long. It is a pleasant, quiet and easily accessible float.

Camping   The nearest camping is at Crater Lake Camp (*see Crater Lake "Camping", previous page*).

Directions   From Interstate 5 in Redding take Hwy 36 east toward Lassen National Park, continue on Hwy 36 past the town of Chester and Lake Almanor to the town of Westwood, from Westwood go north on County Road A21 to the junction with Hwy 44, go south on Hwy 44 and keep an eye out on the right for Long Lake, there is no marked turnoff, you just have to wing it, an unmarked dirt road leads to the lake.

Resources   Lassen National Forest map from USFS, Pine Creek Valley and Swain Mountain topo maps from USGS.

Advisory   Listen to your mother, use sunscreen. Snows make the lake inaccessible in winter.

Information   Lassen National Forest: 530-257-2151

The Moon rises over marshy Long Lake

Wilson Lake

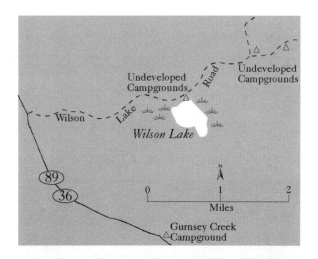

Description   Wilson Lake sits at about 5,200 feet elevation near the south end of Lassen National Park. It's a more or less undiscovered lake. It's a small, natural lake that's perfect for canoeing. Lots of water grasses and plants keep any motors off the lake. You'll usually have the place all to yourself.

Camping   There are a few undeveloped campsites around the lake with no tables, no toilets and no water, no fee, no reservations. Basically, no nothin' but a place to put a tent next to the lake. Nearby Gurnsey Creek campground has 32 sites with tables, fireplaces, toilets and piped water for a fee, no reservations.

Directions   From the junction of Hwy 36/89 just south of Lassen National Park, go south and east about 5 miles and look for the street sign for Wilson Lake Rd. on the east side of the highway, drive east on Wilson Lake Road about 2.5 miles to the lake and campgrounds. It helps to have a Lassen National Forest map.

Resources   Lassen National Forest Map, Childs Meadows topo map from USGS.

Advisory   There is a leviathan living at the east end of the lake. Just kidding. Winter snows make the lake inaccessible in winter.

Information   Lassen National Forest, 530-257-2151

Gliding through the water plants on Wilson Lake

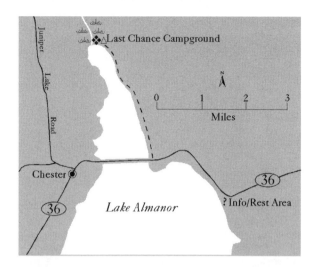

Big, big Lake Almanor

Pelicans nest near Last Chance Campground

Lake Almanor

Description
Lake Almanor is a huge lake with over 28,000 acres of water. It is 6 miles wide and 13 miles long. It sits at 4,500 feet and is surrounded by pine trees. Even though this is a man-made lake built by PG&E, it has the feel of a natural lake. It is kept full year-round and the water is a beautiful, clear blue. There is also a great view of snow-capped Mount Lassen. This is a very popular lake during the summer months and there is usually a lot of power boat traffic. The best canoeing is at the very north end of the lake near Last Chance Creek Campground. It's a somewhat marshy area and there is no power boat traffic. White pelicans nest in this area of the lake.

Camping
There are many campgrounds and resorts around the lake. Last Chance Creek is a PG&E campground that is the closest camp to the canoeable part of the lake. It has 12 sites with water, outhouse toilets, tables and fireplaces for a fee, no reservations.

Directions
From the town of Chester on Hwy 36 go east a little over 2 miles to the Last Chance Campground turnoff just past the east side of the causeway that goes over Lake Almanor, go north for about 4 miles to the campground. Access is at the campground where Last Chance Creek empties into Lake Almanor. In late summer when the water level goes down, it can be a ways from the camp to the lake.

Resources
Lassen National Forest map, Chester USGS topo map

Advisory
There is a lot of power boat traffic. If you venture onto the main lake, stay near the shore. The lake is subject to howling winds, especially in the spring. They can come up quickly, churning the lake into a frothy mass. Very dangerous for canoes. Again, stay near the shore just in case. The area can get a lot of snow in the winter and even freeze the lake surface.

Information
Pacific Gas & Electric Regional Land Department.: 530-529-6316, Chester-Lake Almanor Chamber of Commerce 530-258-2426, Plumas County Chamber of Commerce 800-326-2247 or 530-283-6345, or the Lassen National Forest Lake Almanor Office 530-258-2141

Mountain Meadow Reservoir

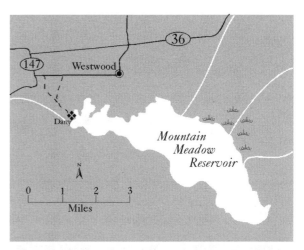

Description   Mountain Meadow Reservoir is a good sized lake with some really nice marshy areas to explore in your canoe. This natural looking man-made reservoir is unknown to everyone except the locals. The main part of the lake is used mostly by local fisherman with small motors. The reservoir sits at 4,500 feet elevation and is surrounded by forests and marshes. It's about 6 miles long and a mile and a half wide at it's widest. There are some hiking trails around parts of the lake.

Camping   There is no camping at Mountain Meadow Reservoir. The nearest campground is at Last Chance Camp (*see Lake Almanor, "Camping", previous page*).

Directions   From the town of Chester on Hwy 36 go east to the junction with Hwy 147, go south on Hwy 147 less than a mile to Mooney Road, go east on Mooney Road about a quarter of a mile, look on the south side of Mooney Road for a dirt road, take that road to the lake.

Resources   Lassen National Forest map from USFS - Westwood West, Westwood East and Greenville topo maps from USGS.

Advisory   Winds can get very strong. Stay near shore. Winter snows make the lake inaccessible.

Information   Plumas County Chamber of Commerce 800-326-2247 or 530-283-6345, or the Lassen National Forest Lake Almanor Office 530-258-2141

One of the marshy areas of Mountain Meadow Reservoir

Cattails cover the shoreline

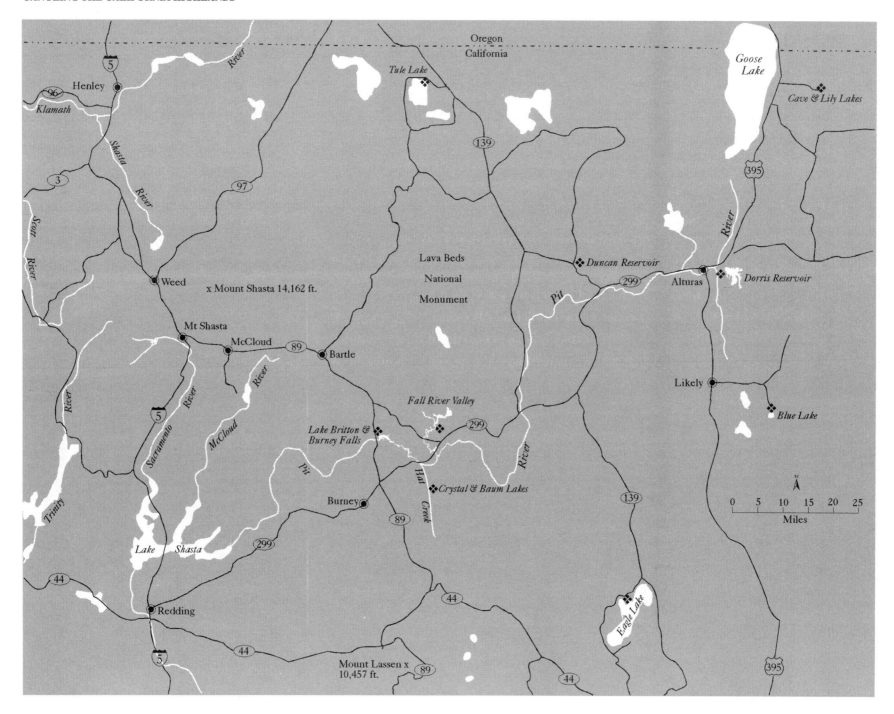

The Modoc Plateau

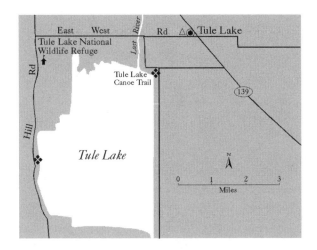

Tule Lake

Description Tule Lake is considered a canoe area and has a marked canoe trail that meanders through the tules at the northeast corner of the lake. The other put-in on the west side of the lake brings you out into more open water. Tule Lake National Wildlife Refuge has one of the largest concentrations of migratory waterfowl in the world where more than 275 kinds of birds have been identified. This area is part of the Klamath Basin Wildlife Refuge, the largest area in the lower 48 states for wintering bald eagles. This is paradise for wildlife photographers and observers. Nearby Lower Klamath and Clear Lakes allow boats only during hunting season.

Camping Although it is about 25 miles from Tule Lake, Indian Wells campground is a great place to stay. A day can be spent just exploring the Lava Beds National Monument around Indians Wells. There are lava tube caves, Indian pictographs, a climable cinder cone, Mammoth Crater and not a whole lot of shade (except in the caves). During the summer season the 40 campsites have water and flush toilets, as well as tables and fireplaces for a fee, no reservations. During the fall and winter they turn off the water, but still have pit toilets, and water is available at the park headquarters, winter camping is free.

 If you want to stay closer to the lake or if Indian Wells is full you can stay at either Stateline RV Park or the Shady Lanes Trailer Park in the town of Tulelake. Not real pretty places, but you can pitch a tent and they do have fireplaces, showers and flush toilets for a fee, reservations accepted.

Directions From Interstate 5 in Weed take Hwy 97 north to the junction with Hwy 161, go east on Hwy 161 to Hill Road, go south on Hill Road 4 miles to the Tule Lake Visitor's Center. To get to the canoe trail put-in: from the Tule Lake Visitor's Center go north on Hill Road to East West Road, go east on East West Road to unmarked road on the east side of the Lost River bridge, go south on the dirt road to the first right you can make, continue south to the canoe trail put-in. Indian Wells campground is about 30 miles south of Tule Lake off Hill Road.

Resources Modoc National Forest map from the USFS, Hatfield and Tule Lake topo maps from the USGS

Advisory If you don't like guns, avoid Tule Lake during hunting season. Bring your own water or a water filter in the off season.

Information Klamath Basin National Wildlife Refuge: 530-667-2231, Tule Lake Chamber of Commerce: 530-667-5178

The Tule Lake Canoe Trail

Duncan Reservoir

Description Duncan Reservoir is a small, natural looking lake that truly deserves the description "pretty". You won't break any distance records here, but you sure can have a pleasant float. Duncan Reservoir rests on the lava flows at about 4,700 feet elevation and is surrounded by dwarf forests and delicate water plants. It's easily accessible off the highway.

Camping Howard's Gulch campground is located three miles south of Duncan Reservoir on the south side of Hwy 139 just east of Loveness Road. It has 11 sites with tables, fireplaces and toilets and no water for a fee, no reservations.

Directions From Tule Lake go east on Hwy 139 to Loveness Road 6 miles west of the town of Canby, go north on Loveness Road (Forest Service Road 46) about one quarter mile north to Forest Service Road 40N06, go east on 40N06 a little over 1 mile to Forest Service Road 46N06A, go north on 46N06A to the lake. It's easier that it sounds.

Resources Modoc National Forest map from USFS, Ambrose topo map from USGS.

Advisory Bring your own water.

Information Modoc National Forest Office: 530-233-5811

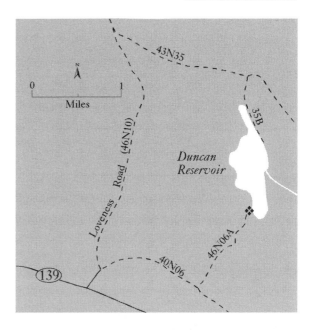

Duncan Reservoir sits in a lava bed bowl

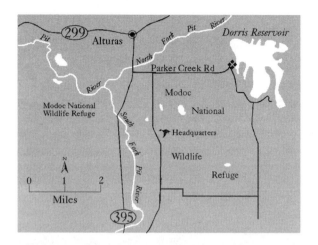

Dorris Reservoir

Description   Although this is not the prettiest lake I've ever seen, as part of the Modoc National Wildlife Refuge, Dorris Reservoir has an abundance of wildlife, especially water fowl. The reservoir sits at about 4,900 feet elevation. It's a good sized body of water that's used mostly by fishermen, although water skiing is allowed. The lake is only open to boating from April 1st through September 30th and closes every night at 8pm. Bring your camera or binoculars and check out the birds.

Camping   Convenient camping is very sparse in this area. Howard's Gulch is your best bet (*see Duncan Reservoir, "Camping", previous page*). The nearby town of Alturas has some inexpensive motels.

Directions   From Hwy 395 at the south end of the town of Alturas, take Parker Creek Road (marked Dorris Reservoir) about 3 miles east, go north at the fork to the reservoir boat ramp.

Resources   Modoc National Forest map, Dorris Reservoir topo map from USGS.

Advisory   The reservoir is only open April through September and closes at 8pm in the summer. Winds can get quite strong. Watch for power boats. Bring your own water.

Information   Modoc National Wildlife Refuge: 530-233-3572

Waterfowl abounds in the Modoc National Wildlife Refuge

Dorris Reservoir

Lily & Cave Lakes

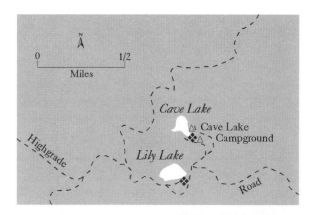

Description These two natural mountain lakes sit right next to each other at 6,600 feet in the very northeasternmost corner of California. We're talkin' beautifully remote, rarely used and exquisitely quiet. Lily Lake is actually covered with lily pads that bloom in early summer. Both lakes are small, but they make for a very pleasant vacation. There are lots of wildflowers in July and August. Motors of any kind are prohibited on the lakes.

Camping There are six campsites at Cave Lake with water, tables, fireplaces and vault toilets and piped water, no fee, no reservations. Open from July to October.

Directions Take Hwy 395 north out of Alturas to Highgrade Road near the Oregon border; go east on Highgrade Road for about 6.5 miles to the lakes.

Resources Modoc National Forest map from the USFS; Willow Ranch topo map from the USGS

Advisory The road is fairly steep, so trailers are not advised; not for timid drivers. Winter snow makes the lakes inaccessible. Bring your own water

Information Warner Mountain Ranger District; 530-279-6119

Lily Lake really is covered with lily pads

Cave Lake

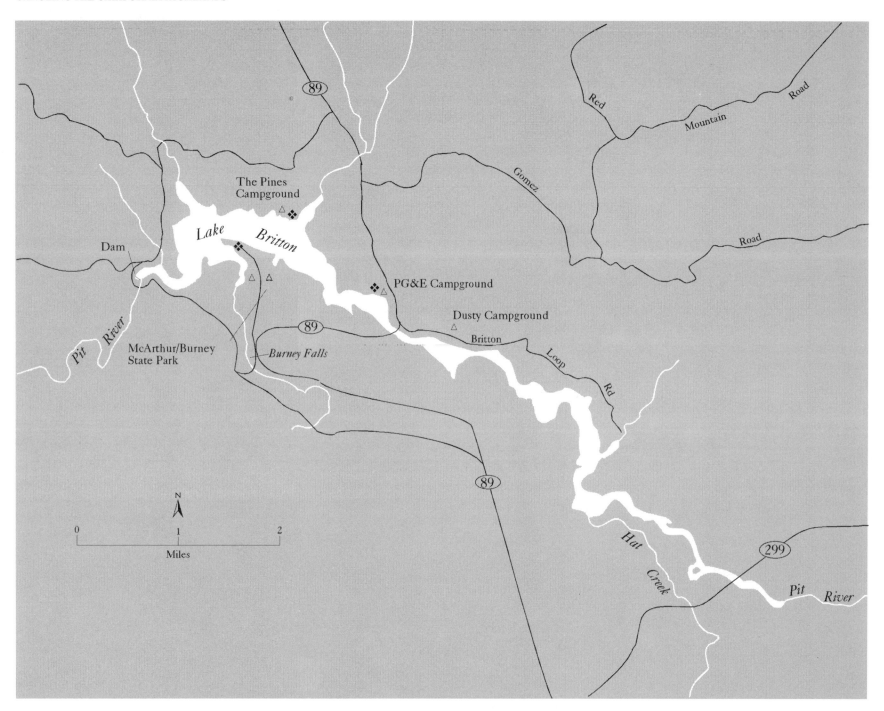

Lake Britton

Description In a landscape of lush evergreen forests and lava flows, Lake Britton is a man made lake sitting at 2,760 feet with 18 miles of shoreline. The best canoeing is up the Pit River/Hat Creek end of the lake. Don't miss Burney Falls up at the end of Burney Creek. This 129 foot double waterfall cascades down over basalt rock in the midst of a beautiful riparian corridor. After the spring rains, Burney Falls really put on a show and the lake is full. Besides paddling, Lake Britton offers many hiking opportunities. The Pacific Crest Trail is nearby, as well as trails to the spectacular views of Burney Spring Mountain and Long Valley Mountain. There is also an abundance of wildlife to look for, including black swifts and swallows darting to their nests behind the falls; bald eagles, double crested cormorants fishing the lake, as well as great blue herons, skunks, woodpeckers, owls and belted kingfishers.

Camping McArthur/Burney Falls Memorial State Park has 128 campsites with piped water, tables, fireplaces, flush toilets and showers for a fee, reservations through Destinet: 800-444-7275. Along the north shore of the lake PG&E maintains some campgrounds with 30 campsites with water, tables, fireplaces, and vault toilets for a fee, no reservations. Dusty campground has 7 undeveloped sites with tables, fireplaces, toilets and no water for a fee, no reservations.

Directions From Hwy 299 in Burney go east 5 miles to the junction with Hwy 89, go about 4.5 miles north on 89 to the entrance to McArthur/Burney Falls Memorial Park. There are boat ramps at both campgrounds.

Resources Shasta Trinity National Forest map from the USFS, Burney Falls and Dana topo maps from the USGS, brochure from McArthur/Burney Falls State Park office.

Advisory This is a very popular spot and quite crowded in the summer. Try to visit it in the off season.Watch for power boats and jet skis. Bring your own water to some of the campgrounds.

Information McArthur/Burney Falls State Park: 530-335-2777

The Pit River enters Lake Britton on a windless morning

Spectacular Burney Falls

Ja She Creek Area © *California State Parks*

Horr Pond © *California State Parks*

Mount Shasta looms behind the Fall River Valley © *California State Parks*

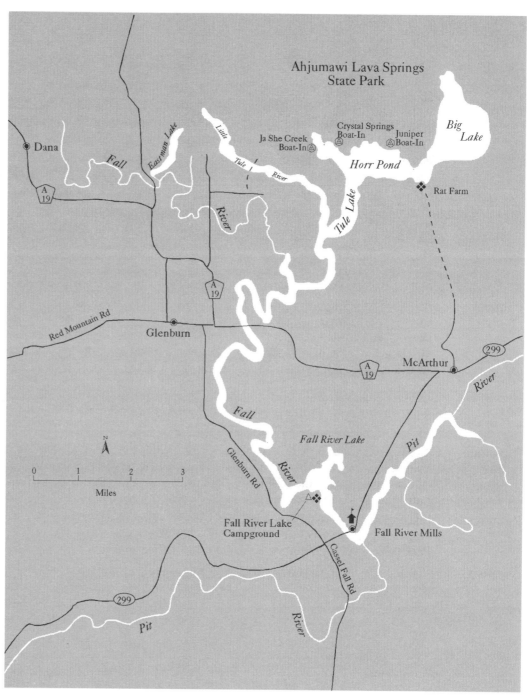

Fall River Valley

Description
This is one of the premier canoeing spots in all of California, with gorgeous scenery, abundant wildlife and paddle-in camping.The Fall River Valley sits at about 3000 feet elevation between the Sierra and Cascade mountain ranges. The valley is filled with the meanderings of the Fall, Little Tule and Pit Rivers.The Ahjumawi Lava Springs State Park rests at the north end of the Fall River Valley just above Big Lake. The State Park brochure describes it perfectly: "Ahjumawi is a place of exceptional, even primeval, beauty. Brilliant aqua bays and tree studded islets only a few yards long dot the shore line of Horr Pond and Ja She Creek. Of the park's 6000 acres, over two thirds of the area is covered by recent lava flows including vast areas of jagged black basalt. It is a place of natural wonder only minimally marked by man." The entire area is ideal for wildlife viewing and photography (I saw an osprey dive into the water for lunch, WOW!). Big Lake, Horr Pond, Tule Lake, the Little Tule River and Eastman Lake are all contiguous. There is a 10 mph speed limit throughout the area. Nearby is Lake Britton and Burney Falls *(see previous page)*.

Camping
Primitive camping is available at nine Enviromental Campsites. There are three each located near Ja She creek, at Crystal Springs and on the north shore of Horr Pond with pit toilets, and fire rings, and can only be reached by boat. Water is available from the many springs, but must be purified. A camping fee is charged and camping is allowed only in the designated areas. Pets are allowed but strongly discouraged. PG&E has built a campground with 20 sites near the town of Cassel about one mile south of Lake Baum. McArthur/Burney Falls Memorial State Park has 28 developed sites and PG&E has 36 sites, both at Lake Britton about 12 miles from Fall River Mills.

Directions
Take Hwy 299 to McArthur, turn north onto Main St., go past the Intermountain Fairgrounds, cross over a canal and proceed three miles north on Rat Ranch Road (graded dirt road) to the boat ramp. Park and put-in at the PG&E public boat ramp known as "the Rat Farm".

Resources
Shasta/Trinity National Forest map from USFS - Timbered Crater, Fall River Mills, Hogback Ridge USGS Topo maps - brochure for Ahjumawi Lava Springs State Park from McArthur/Burney Falls State Park office.

Advisory
If you don't like guns stay away during hunting season. Bring your own water. You may want to bring a bug suit, as the mosquitos can be horrendous.

Information
McArthur/Burney Falls Memorial State Park: 530-335-2777

Mount Shasta looms above Horr Pond

Ahjumawi-Lava Springs State Park   © *California State Parks*

Crystal Lake on a calm day

Pastoral Baum Lake

Crystal & Baum Lakes

Description   The best way to describe Crystal and Baum Lakes is pastoral, complete with cows. They are both small, Crystal Lake at 60 acres and Baum Lake at 89 acres. They rest at about 3,000 feet elevation in the Shasta National Forest surrounded by forests and meadows. Motors of any kind are prohibited on both lakes assuring a level of tranquility perfect for floating around in a canoe.

Camping   Cassel campground has 27 sites with table, fireplaces, toilets and piped water for a fee, no reservations.

Directions   From Interstate 5 just north of Redding take the Hwy 299 East exit, go east on Hwy 299 past the town of Burney to the junction of Hwy 299 and Hwy 89, continue straight on Hwy 299 for 2 miles to Cassel Road, go south on Cassel Road for 2.5 miles to the Hat Creek/Power House Road, go east on Hat Creek/Power House Road to the lakes. Baum Lake is easy to find. For Crystal Lake, turn north onto a dirt off Hat Creek/Powerhouse Road to a dirt parking lot, portage your canoe about 100 yards to the lake. Cassel campground is about 1 mile further south past Hat Creek/Power House Road on Cassel Road off to the left.

Resources   Shasta or Lassen National Forest map from USFS, Cassel topo map from USGS.

Advisory   Swimming is strictly prohibited in either lake and Hat Creek.

Information   Pacific Gas & Electric: 800-743-5000

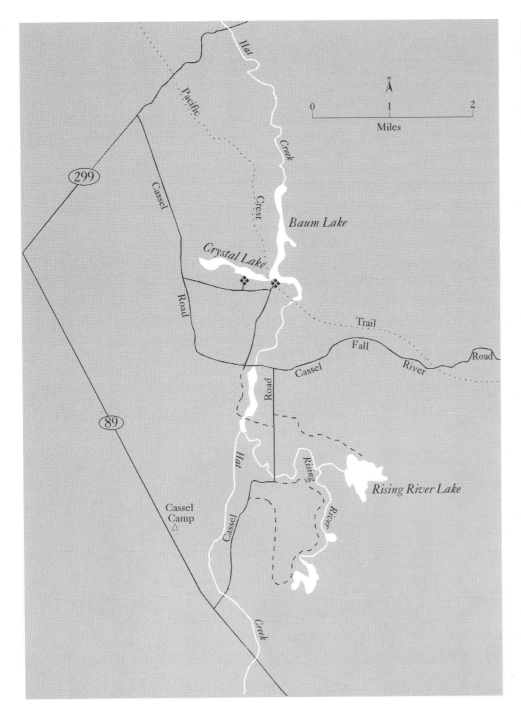

Baum Lake

Crystal Lake on Hat Creek

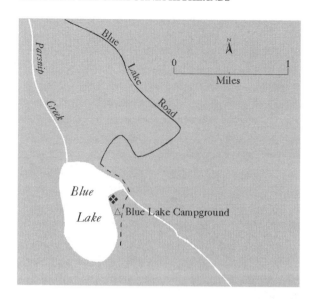

Blue Lake

Description	Situated in the Warner Mountains at 6,000 feet elevation, Blue Lake is a beautiful small lake, 160 acres. It's surrounded by forests of ponderosa pine and white fir. Although the lake is fairly remote, it does get quite a bit of summer vacation traffic. Power boats are allowed on the lake, but it's a bit too small for water skiing and a 5 m.p.h speed limit is enforced. Most of the use is by fishermen with small-motored boats. There is an easy trail around the lake. Bald Eagles can be spotted here in spring and early S\summer.
Camping	Blue Lake campground has 48 sites with tables, fireplaces, toilets and piped water for a fee, no reservations.
Directions	From the town of Alturas go south on Hwy 395 17 miles to the town of Likely, go east on Jess Valley Road (County Road 64) about 8.5 miles to Blue Lake Road, go south on Blue Lake Road about 7 miles to Forest Service Road 39N30, take 39N30 to the lake and campground.
Resources	Modoc National Forest map from USFS, Jess Valley topo map from USGS.
Advisory	Campground is closed November through May. Winter snow makes the lake inaccessible.
Information	Modoc National Forest: 530-279-6116

Beautiful Blue Lake

Eagle Lake

Description   Eagle Lake is the second largest natural lake in California, with 27,000 surface acres of warm clear water and more than 100 miles of shoreline. It sits at 5,100 feet in the Lassen National Forest. The southern shore is forested with pine and cedar, while the northern shore is dominated by sage and juniper. The lake attracts many fish eating birds including bald eagles, osprey, and white pelicans; as well as ducks, egrets, common teal and other shore feeding waterfowl. In fact, the western shore is an osprey management area. The open lake is a little too open for canoes and power boats and jet skis are very popular. I like Fred's Road for a canoe put-in.

Camping   All these campgrounds have tables, fireplaces, piped water and flush toilets for a fee: Christie, 69 sites, no reservations - Merrill 181 sites, no reservations - Eagle 50 sites, reserve through Destinet: 800-444-7275 - Aspen Grove 26 sites for tent only, no reservations.

Directions   From Susanville take Highway 36 west, go north on Eagle Lake Road (Road A10) about 14 miles to the south end of the lake, follow the signs to the campground of your choice.

Resources   Lassen National Forest map from USFS; Spalding Tract, Troxel Point, Pikes Point and Gallatin Peak topo maps from USGS

Advisory   Keep an eye out for power boats. Watch for afternoon winds and stay away from the middle of the lake, it's a long swim to shore.

Information   Lassen National Forest, 530-257-2151

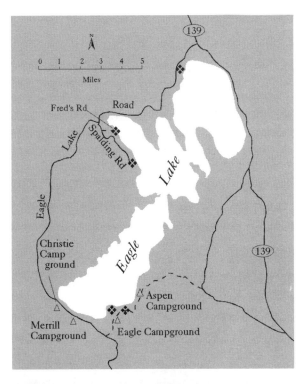

Cirrus clouds dancing above Eagle Lake

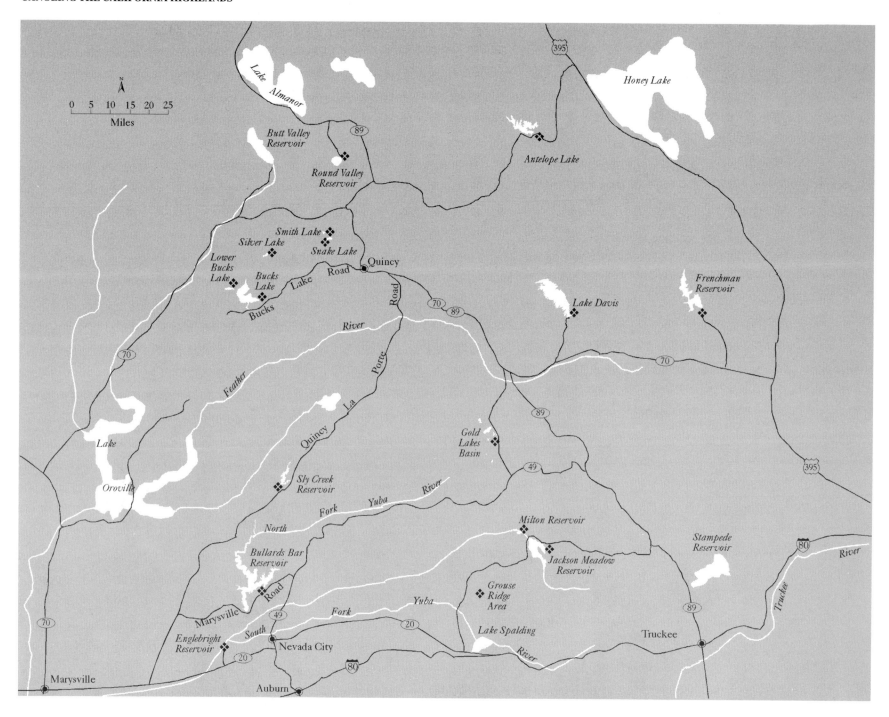

The Northern Sierra

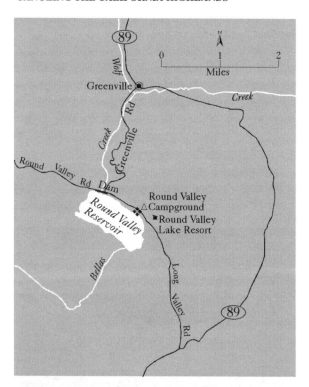

Round Valley Reservoir

Description   Round Valley Lake rests at 4,500 feet surrounded by large pines in the Plumas National Forest. Since this is a warm water lake there is more water born vegetation including lily pads. This is a small reservoir used mainly by fishermen seeking black bass and catfish. The area also plays host to nesting bald eagles, osprey and other alpine wildlife. Only small fishing motors are allowed on the lake, so big wakes are not a problem. The folks who run the resort are real nice. Open May through September (more or less).

Camping   There are 50 sites with running water, flush toilets, fireplaces, tables and showers for a fee, reservations through Round Valley Resort, *(see information, below)*.

Directions   From Hwy 89 in Greenville go south on Round Valley Road about 3 miles to the lake and about 1 mile more to the campground.

Resources   Plumas National Forest map from USFS, Crescent Mill topo map from USGS, pamphlet from Round Valley Resort *(see information, below)*.

Advisory   As the water supply for the town of Greenville, no swimming is allowed.

Information   Round Valley Resort: 530-284-7978 or 714-637-3181

Peaceful paddling on Round Valley Reservoir

Antelope Lake

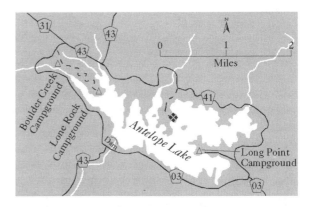

Description   Antelope Lake sits at 5000 feet elevation among the pines and firs of the northern Sierra Nevada Range. There are 15 miles of shoreline with many coves and several islands to explore. This is a gorgeous lake ideal for canoeing. Although water skiing and jet skis are allowed on the lake, their domain is the deeper waters in the middle of the lake. If you stick to the shoreline you can have a great paddle among the wildlife. More than a half dozen creeks feed Antelope Lake where waterfowl including gadwalls, mallards, common mergansers, grebes, and cinnamon teal nest among the many protected coves. Beaver can be seen if you sit quietly near their dam homes upstream on Little Antelope Creek. The creeks all have wet meadows on their banks which attract wildlife aplenty including warbling vireos, great blue heron, wood ducks and black bears. Osprey pairs and bald eagles can be seen nesting in tree tops. If you can get up a little before sunrise, you can treat yourself to a paddle through the early morning mist that often hovers above the lake.

Camping   Long Point, 38 sites and Lone Rock, 86 sites sit right on the lake with water, toilets, tables and fireplaces for a fee, reservations through Destinet: 800-444-7275. Open May through October.

Directions   Take Hwy 89 to Road A22 to Taylorsville, from Taylorville go east on Genesee Road to the town of Genesee, go east on Beckwourth-Indian Creek Road to the lake. There are boat ramps at the campgrounds.

Resources   Antelope Lake topo map from the USGS, Plumas National Forest map from the USFS.

Advisory   Snow can make the lake inaccessible.

Information   Greenville Ranger District: 530-284-7126

Sunrise mists on Antelope Lakes

One of Antelope Lake's many quiet coves

Paddle among the water plants on Snake Lake

Isolated Smith Lake

Bucks Lake Area

Description   The Bucks Lake Area offers five very different lakes to explore by canoe. Bucks Lake is the biggest with 1,827 surface acres at 5,153 feet elevation. Bucks Lake is a recreational lake with lots of power boats and jet skis, but you can do some distance paddling. Lower Bucks Lake sits below the dam of Bucks Lake. It's quieter and gets much less traffic than it's upper brother. There's a very pictur-esque cascade where Bucks Creek enters the lake. Snake Lake is a pretty lake that sits at 4,200 feet elevation. No motors are allowed on Snake Lake and it gets covered with a plant called water shield which is fun to paddle through. Some-times they close the lake because of the plant. Smith Lake is rarely visited by anyone. It has it's own beauty and you will often be the only one there. Smith Lake also prohibits motors and get covered with water shield. Silver Lake is an incredibly beautiful lake located at 5,800 feet elevation. Motors of any kind are prohibited on Silver Lake which makes it ideal for paddling.

Camping   All theses camps have tables, fireplaces and toilets for a fee, no reservations. Mill Creek: 8 sites, piped water, flush toilets - Sundew: 19 sites, piped water - Hanskins: 65 sites, piped water - White Horse: 20 sites, piped water - Lower Bucks Lake: 6 sites, no toilets, no water - Snake Lake: 7 sites for tents only, no water, no fee - Silver Lake: 7 sites for tents only, no water, no fee.

Directions   All lakes: from Hwy 89 in Quincy go west on Bucks Lake Road. Snake Lake: 5 miles west of Quincy go north on County Road 422 for about 2 miles to the Snake Lake access road, go east on the access road 1 mile to the lake and camp-ground. Smith Lake: stay on County Road 422 go straight past the Snake Lake access road about 1.5 miles to the Smith Lake access road, go west on the access road to the lake. Silver Lake: 9 miles west of Quincy in the town of Spanish Ranch go north on Silver Lake Road to the campground and lake. Bucks Lake: 17 miles west of Quincy is the lake and campgrounds. Lower Bucks Lake: just past Bucks Lake dam go west on Lower Bucks Lake access road to the lake and campground.

Resources   Plumas National Forest map from USFS - Buck's Lake, Meadow Valley, and Hanskins Valley topo maps from USGS.

Advisory   Bring your own water to Lower Bucks, Silver, Smith and Snake Lakes. Winter snows make this area inaccessible. Watch for power boats on Bucks Lake.

Information   Plumas National Forest: 530-283-2050.

Tiny Thompson Lake

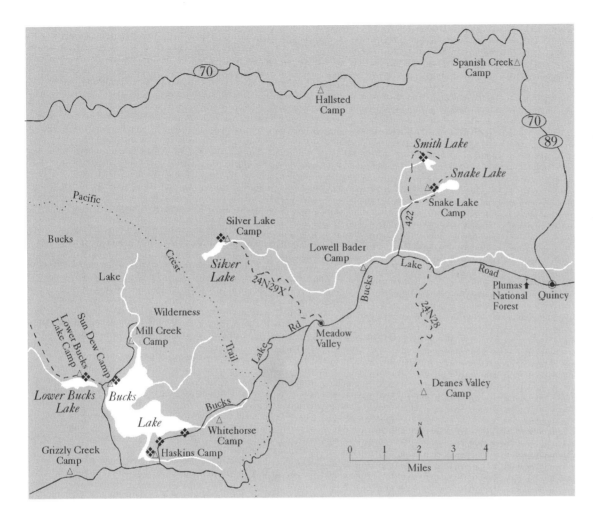

Sunrise on Silver Lake

Bucks Lake offers some long distance paddling

Bucks Creek enters Lower Bucks Lake

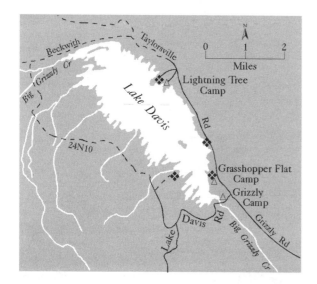

Lake Davis

Description Lake Davis is a good-sized lake which lies at 5,775 feet elevation with 4,026 surface acres of water surrounded by rolling, grassy meadows and pines. There are 32 miles of shoreline and many little coves to explore with delicate streams emptying into the lake. The Smith Peak Lookout has a great view of the lake and surrounding area. Wildlife sightings include bald eagles in spring and fall, ospreys in the summer, white pelicans, nuthatches and herons.

In 1997 the Department of Fish and Game poisoned the lake to kill off a predatory fish, the northern pike, that was decimating the game fish population. Lake Davis is the drinking water source for the town of Portola. A great controversy still rages. All the fish in the lake were killed and the game fish were restocked. As of this writing there was still some chemical residue in the water, but Fish and Game says it's safe. Some people have their doubts. Believe who you will, it's still a pretty lake.

Camping These two campgrounds have tables, fireplaces, flush toilets and piped water for a fee, no reservations: Grasshopper Flat, 70 sites - Grizzly, 55 sites. Lightning Tree campground has 38 sites with tables and fireplaces, no water, no toilets, no fee and no reservations.

Directions From Interstate 80 at Truckee take the 89 north exit, go north on Hwy 89 to the junction with Hwy 70, go east on Hwy 70 to the town of Portola, from Portola go north on Lake Davis Road to the lake and campgrounds.

Resources Plumas National Forest map from the USFS, Grizzly Valley and Crocker Mountain topo maps from the USGS.

Advisory This lake can be very crowded in the summer months. Watch out for power boats. Winds can be strong in the afternoon. Snow makes the lake inaccessible.

Information Plumas National Forest: 9530-836-2575

Lake Davis from the dam

Brown pelicans nest at Lake Davis

Frenchman Reservoir

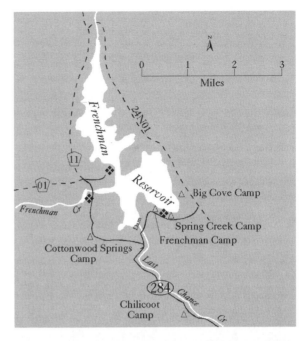

Description   Frenchman Reservoir is a big lake resting at 5,588 feet elevation surrounded on the west by pine forests and on the east with high sage desert. The lake covers 1,580 acres with 21 miles of shoreline and offers some good long distance paddling opportunities and some secluded coves to explore. This lake gets a lot of power boat and jet ski traffic in the summer. The afternoon winds come screaming down from the crest of the Sierra Nevada and into the high Nevada desert. You're best off staying near shore. In late spring and early summer when the lake level is high, there is a nice side trip paddling up Frenchman Creek on the west side of County Road 11.

Camping   All these campgrounds have tables, fireplaces, toilets and piped water for a fee, reserve through Destinet: 800-444-7275: Cottonwood Springs, 20 sites, flush toilets - Frenchman, 38 sites - Big Cove, 38 sites (11 are wheelchair accessible), flush toilets - Spring Cove, 35 sites.

Directions   From Interstate 80 at Truckee take the 89 north exit, go north on Hwy 89 to the junction with Hwy 49 in Sierraville, go east and north on Hwy 49 to the junction with Hwy 70, go east on Hwy 70 to Frenchman Lake Road, go north on Frenchman Lake Road (Hwy 284) to the lake and campgrounds. The road in parallels Little Last Chance Creek which cuts a canyon through basalt rock making for a very pretty drive.

Resources   Plumas National Forest map from the USFS.

Advisory   This lake can be very crowded in the summer months. Watch out for power boats. Afternoon winds really rip. Stay near shore.

Information   Plumas National Forest: 530-836-2575

One of many coves on Frenchman Reservoir

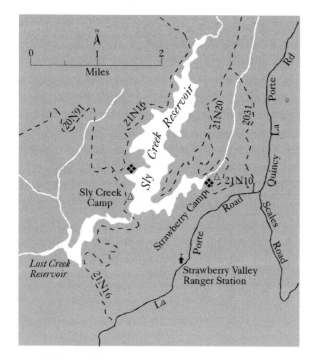

Sly Creek enters Sly Creek Reservoir

Sly Creek Reservoir

Description   Sly Creek Reservoir is a long, narrow lake that sits at 3,560 feet evelation in the Plumas National Forest. This small lake (562 acres) is an ideal paddling getaway. When I was there in late October the water level was down about 40 feet. The shoreline was striated with parallel lines which were reflecting perfectly in the still water. From an artistic design point of view it was very pretty. Power boats and jet skis are prohibited on Sly Creek Reservoir. You can really get the strokes going on this 3 miles long lake and you don't have to worry about getting run over.

Camping   Both these campgrounds have piped water, tables, fireplaces and toilets for a fee, no reservations: Sly Creek, 14 sites - Strawberry, 15 sites.

Directions   From Hwy 70 in Marysville go east on Hwy 20 about 12 miles to Marysville Road, go north on Marysville Road, Marysville Road turn east just past Collins Lake, at the Marysville Road turnoff continue north on Willow Glen Road until it merges with La Porte Road, continue on past the towns of Brownsville, Challenge and Clipper Mills to just before the town of Strawberry Valley, look for the signed turn off to Sly Creek Reservoir, go north on the Sly Creek access road (Forest Service Road 16) about three miles to the lake and campground. It's easier than it sounds.

Resources   Plumas National Forest map from USFS, Strawberry Valley topo map from USGS.

Advisory   Whatever it is, don't let it get you down. Go out into nature. You'll feel better.

Information   Plumas National Forest: 530-534-6500

Little Grass Valley Reservoir

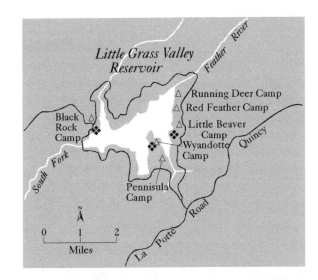

Description   Little Grass Valley Reservoir sits at 5,040 feet elevation on the South Fork Feather River in the Plumas National Forest. At 1,600 surface acres the lake is good-sized. Water skiing and jet skis are allowed but the lake is used mostly by fishermen trolling along at slow speeds hoping to catch that big lunker down in the bottom. In late spring and early summer, when the lake is full, Little Grass Valley Reservoir is very pretty. By late summer, the water level can go way down and it's little more than a puddle with a bad case of reserevoir ring. If you make it out to Sly Creek Reservoir (*previous page*) you might as well check out Little Grass Valley Reservoir.

Camping   All these campground have tables, fireplaces, flush toilets and piped water for a fee: Black Rock, 30 sites (10 walk-in tent sites), no reservations - Wyandotte, 28 sites, no reservations - Little Beaver, 120 sites, no reservations - Red Feather, 60 sites, reservations through 800-280-2267 - Running Deer, 40 sites, no reservations.

Directions   From Hwy 70 in Marysville go east on Hwy 20 about 12 miles to Marysville Road, go north on Marysville Road, Marysville Road turns east just past Collins Lake, at the Marysville Road turnoff continue north on Willow Glen Road until it merges with La Porte Road, continue on past the towns of Brownsville, Challenge, Clipper Mills, Strawberry Valley and Eagleville, just past Eagleville, La Porte Road becomes La Porte-Quincy Road, follow the signs for Quincy and go northeast on La Porte-Quincy Road just past the town of La Porte to the Little Grass Valley Road turnoff (well marked), go northwest on Little Grass Valley Road about three miles to the lake and campgrounds.

Resources   Plumas National Forest map from USFS, American House and La Porte topo maps from USGS.

Little Grass Valley Reservoir has an open feel

Advisory   Summertime can be very crowded. Late summer the water gets pretty low. Winter snows can make the lake inaccessible.

Information   Plumas National Forest: 530-534-6500

Still waters on Little Grass Valley Reservoir

The Sierra Buttes loom high over the Gold Lakes Basin

Cottonwood tree in fall colors at Packer Lake

Lakes Basin Area

Description   The Lakes Basin rests at 5,000-6,000 feet elevation with over 30 crystal clear, snow-fed lakes carved into the glacial granite. There are many lakes in the area that are easy to reach and worthy of paddling including: Gold Lake, Goose Lake, Haven Lake, Snag Lake, Upper Sardine Lake, Lower Salmon Lake and Packer Lake. There are many hiking trails alongside the creeks, streams and lakes that crisscross the Lakes Basin. Plan on spending a few days exploring this area of incredible beauty. Fall is an especially beautiful time in the Lakes Basin area. The leaves are turning gold and red and all the wildlife is scurrying about preparing for winter. Open June through October (more or less).

Camping   All these campgrounds have tables, fireplaces and toilets, no reservations: Lakes Basin, 24 sites, piped water, toilets, for a fee - Gold Lake, a few primitive sites, no water, no fee - Snag Lake, 16 sites, no water, no fee - Pack Saddle, 12 sites, no water - Berger, 10 sites, no water - Diablo, a few primitive sites, no water, no fee - Salmon Creek Sardine Lake, 29 sites, piped water, tables, toilets for a fee. There are also many resorts in the area if you wish to go uptown instead of camping. All facilities and campgrounds open June through October.

Directions   From Interstate 80 at Auburn go north on Hwy 49 to the town of Bassetts, go north on Gold Lake Road to the lakes and campgrounds.

Resources   Tahoe or Plumas National Forest maps from the USFS, Gold Lake topo map from the USGS.

Advisory   Due to snow Lakes Basin is inaccessible in winter. Watch for power boats on Gold Lake. Bring your own water.

Information   For the northern lakes Beckwourth Ranger Station: 530-836-2575; for the southern lakes, Downieville Ranger Station: 530-288-3231.

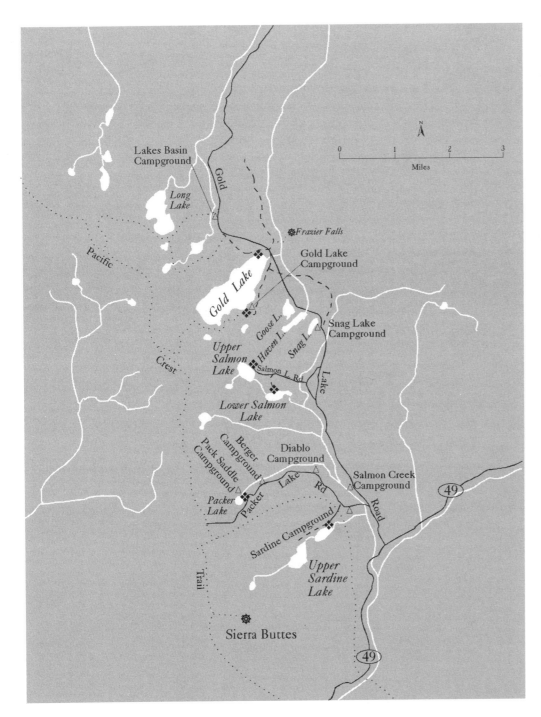

Lakes Basin
Campground

Gold

Long
Lake

Pacific

❀ *Frazier Falls*

Gold Lake
Campground

Gold   Lake

Goose L.

Snag Lake
Campground

*Upper
Salmon
Lake*

Crest

Haven L.

Snag L.

Salmon L. Rd

Lake

*Lower Salmon
Lake*

Berger
Campground

Diablo
Campground

Pack Saddle
Campground

Salmon Creek
Campground

*Packer
Lake*

Packer

Lake

Rd

Road

49

Sardine Campground

Trail

*Upper
Sardine
Lake*

❀
Sierra Buttes

49

N

0   1   2   3

Miles

Cirrus clouds playing tag with the wind over Upper Salmon Lake

Beaver lodge on Lower Salmon Lake

Lower Sardine Lake as seen from Upper Sardine Lake

A placid day on Englebright Reservoir

The watercourse narrows

The South Fork Yuba River enters Englebright Reservoir

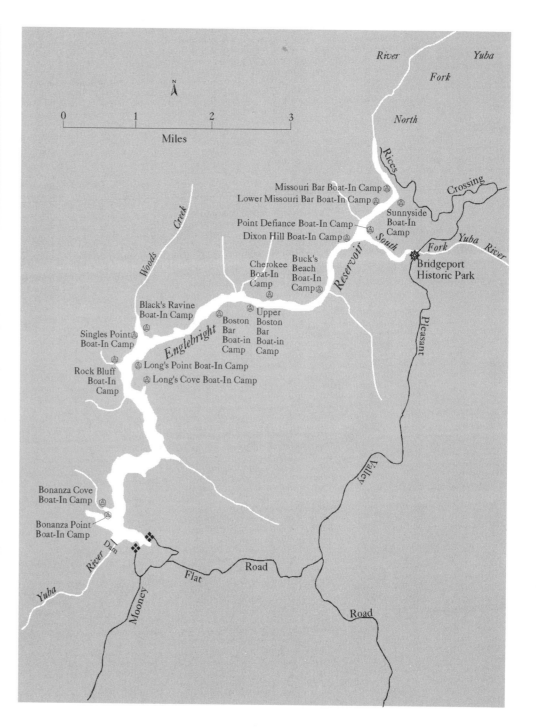

56

Englebright Reservoir

Description: Englebright Reservoir is one of the best lakes for paddle-in camping and long distance canoeing. Englebright Reservoir sits among the pines and oaks of the Sierra Nevada foothills at an elevation of 527 ft. with 815 surface acres. The reservoir is 11 miles long on the Yuba River. Since Englebright sits at such a low elevation with year round, high water levels, it is an ideal lake for winter paddling. This lake is near my home and I go here often in the winter and have the whole place to myself. No water skiing is allowed at the east end of the reservoir past Upper Boston. You can explore the North & South Forks of the Yuba River at the east end of the reservoir. Wildlife is abundant at Englebright. I've seen bald eagles, red-tailed hawks, beaver, deer, and cows (the cows weren't wild, even when they partied).There are many coves to explore along Englebright's shores and most of them have exquisite little creeks and waterfalls to treat you for your paddling efforts.

Camping 17 boat-in camps dot the shoreline, a total of 100 sites all with tables, fireplaces and toilets, no fee, no reservations.

Directions Take Hwy 20 east from Marysville to the Englebright Reservoir turnoff (Mooney Flat Rd) just the other side of Smartville, go three miles to the lake.

Resources Oregon House, Smartville and French Corral USGS topo maps and a brochure from the Corps of Engineers (*see Information below*).

Advisory Watch for power boats. Bring your own water or a water filter. Ocassionally they drain Englebright Reservoir to clean the bottom near the dam. Some campsites close or are hard to reach when water levels are low, call ahead to the Corps of Engineers.

Information U.S.Corps of Engineers: 530-639-2342.

Bald eagles nest at Englebright Reservoir in winter

Ah, the discoveries of exploration

Looking northwest from the air   Courtesy California Dept. of Water Resources

Natural treasures can be found in the coves of Bullards Bar Reservoir

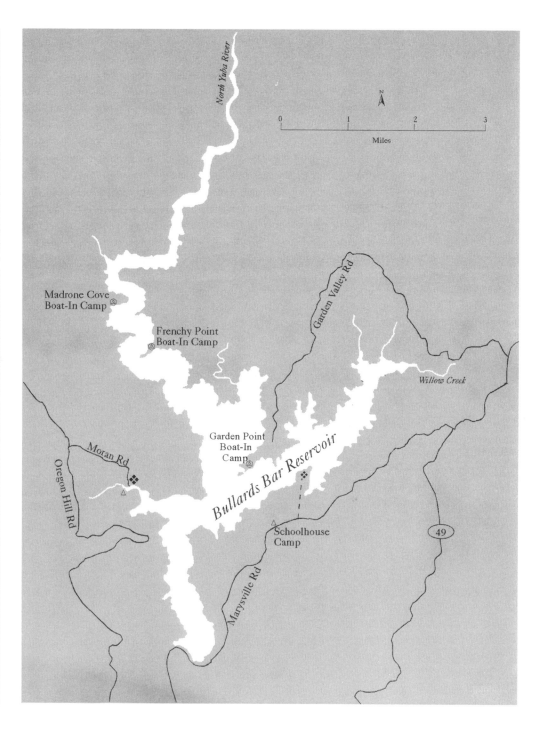

Bullards Bar Reservoir

Description   Bullards Bar Reservoir is a big reservoir (4,700 surface acres) set in the Sierra Nevada Foothills at about 2,000 feet among oak and pine trees. There are 56 miles of shoreline and many coves with year round creeks to explore. There is a beautiful paddle up the North Yuba River where it empties into the reservoir. During the summer months Bullards Bar Reservoir can get really crowded with power boats and jet skis.

The real joys for canoers on this lake are winter paddling (it's open and accessible all year round), long distance paddling, and paddle-in camping. If you're hearty enough to stand the frigid nights, take a few days during a dry spell in winter and paddle up to where the North Fork Yuba River enters the lake, while camping at the paddle-in camps along the way. I've done it. It's a gas and in winter the place is deserted and the water is calm on most cold, clear days.

Camping   There are three boat-in camps with tables, fireplaces and vault toilets: Garden Point, 6 sites - Frency Point, 8 sites - Madrone Cove, 10 sites. You have to pack out your garbage. Reservations and a $7.50 fee per night are required for the boat-in camps (sparse use October-April). Lakeside camping is allowed anywhere you find to your liking as long as you get a permit at the ranger station. No reservations or fees for lakeside camping. If you get to the lake too late to paddle to a boat-in camp try the Schoolhouse campground off Marysville Rd.

Directions   From Interstate 80 at Auburn, take Hwy 49 north to the Hwy 49/20 split at Nevada City, take Hwy 49 north to Camptonville, take Marysville Rd west to Dark Day picnic area/Dark Day boat ramp.

Resources   Tahoe National Forest map from USFS, Challenge and Camptonville USGS topo maps.

Advisory   Watch for power boats. Bring your own water. Some campsites close or are hard to reach when water levels are low, call ahead to the Ranger Station.

Information   Emerald Cove Resort & Marina: 530-692-3200 or North Yuba Ranger Station: 530-288-3231

Exploring a cove

Winter clouds and wind driven swells

Aerial of Bullards Bar   Courtesy California Dept. of Water Resources

Lindsey and Culbertson Lakes from the peak of Fall Creek Mountain

Feely and Carr Lakes from Fall Creek Mountain

Sawmill Lake   *Nory Fussell*

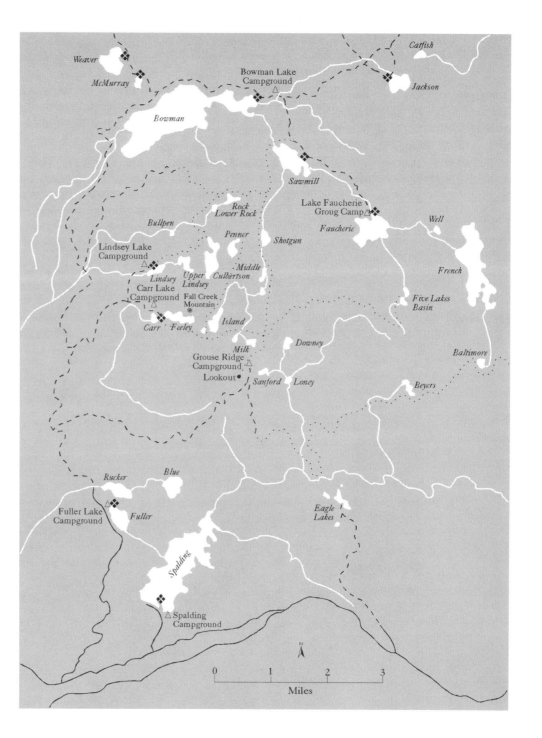

Grouse Ridge Area

Description   There are many beautiful lakes in the Grouse Ridge area that can be reached by car: Fuller, Carr, Feeley, Lindsey, Bowman, McMurray, Weaver, Sawmill and Faucherie Lakes. Except for Bowman Lake, they are all small, elegant lakes. Although the long distance paddler will feel much to be desired, each lake is easily accessible and offers it's own particular mountain feel. There are also many hiking trails in the area worth exploring. For a spectacular view of the area go to the Grouse Ridge Lookout or hike to the top of Fall Creek Mountain on the north side of Feeley Lake.

Camping   Fuller Lake campground has 9 tent campsites with vault toilets, tables and fire rings. Grouse Ridge campground has 9 campsites with water, vault toilets, tables and fire rings. Carr Lake, Feeley Lake, Lindsey Lake, Jackson Creek, Weaver Lake, McMurray Lake and Bowman Lake campgrounds all have some primitive tentsites with fire rings and vault toilets. There are no fees or reservations at any of the campgrounds and none of the campgrounds in the area have piped water so bring your own water or a water filter.

Directions   From the town of Nevada City on Hwy 49/20 take Hwy 20 east toward Truckee to Bowman Lake Road, go north to the lakes and campgrounds.

Resources   Graniteville and English Mountain USGS topo maps, Tahoe National Forest map.

Advisory   Snow storms can hit anytime from October through May. Snow makes the lakes inaccessible. The roads are a little rough, trailers and low riding vehicles not recommended on some roads.

Information   Nevada City Ranger District: 530-265-4531

Mystery Lake?

Safe harbor on Carr Lake

Jackson Meadow & Milton Reservoirs

Description
This pair of beautiful, high mountain lakes offers everything the paddler wants: inspiring natural beauty, awesome vistas, paddle-in camping, long distance paddling and intimate floating.

Jackson Meadow Reservoir lies at 6,200 feet elevation on the Middle Fork of the Yuba River with 11 miles of shore line surrounded by pine forests, grassy meadows and granite peaks. Although water skiing and jet skis are allowed, noise level laws are enforced. Mostly, you'll see a lot of fishermen and great views of the Sierra Buttes.

Milton Reservoir, also along the Middle Fork Yuba River, is a small, intimate jewel of a lake. The atmosphere at Milton is much more laid back than the larger Jackson Meadow. It is always full and lends itself well to the spirit of floating.

Camping
Jackson Meadow Reservoir: all these camps have tables, fireplaces and toilets for a fee, reserve through Destinet: 800-444-7275. Woodcamp, 10 sites, piped water, flush toilets - Pass Creek, 30 sites, piped water - Fir Top, 12 sites, piped water, flush toilets - Findley, 15 sites, piped water, flush toilets - Jackson Point Boat-In, 10 sites, no water.

Directions
From Interstate 80 out of Truckee go approximately 17 miles north on Hwy 89 to a left turn onto Fiberboard Road, take Fiberboard Road all the way to the first boat ramp on Jackson Meadow Reservoir. Along Fiberboard Road on the way in are views of the Little Truckee River valley and outrageous alpine meadows of late spring and summer wildflowers. The Pacific Crest Trail runs right by the reservoir if you wish to do some hiking or backpacking.

Resources
Tahoe National Forest map from USFS, Haypress Valley and English Mountain topo maps from the USGS.

Advisory
Watch for power boats. Bring your own water to Jackson Point Boat-In Camp. Winds can be horrendous on Jackson Meadow Reservoir. Winter snows make the area inaccessible.

Information
Sierraville Ranger Station: 530-994-3401

Sunset behind the Sierra Buttes at Jackson Meadow Reservoir

Jackson Meadow Reservoir offers paddle-in camping

Marshy creeks at the head of Milton Reservoir

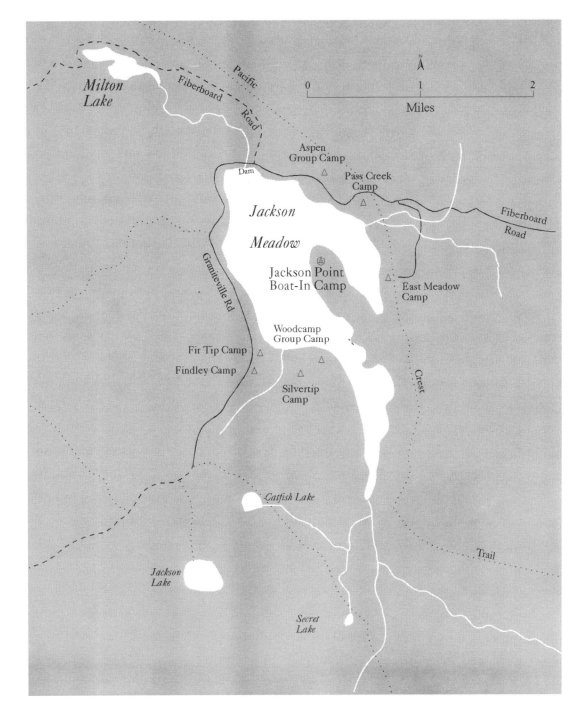

Water plants in shallow water on Milton Reservoir

Small, serene Milton Reservoir

Milton Lake

Fiberboard Road

Pacific

0   1   2

Miles

Aspen Group Camp

Dam

Pass Creek Camp

Jackson

Meadow

Fiberboard Road

Jackson Point Boat-In Camp

East Meadow Camp

Granieville Rd

Woodcamp Group Camp

Fir Tip Camp

Findley Camp

Silvertip Camp

Crest

Catfish Lake

Jackson Lake

Trail

Secret Lake

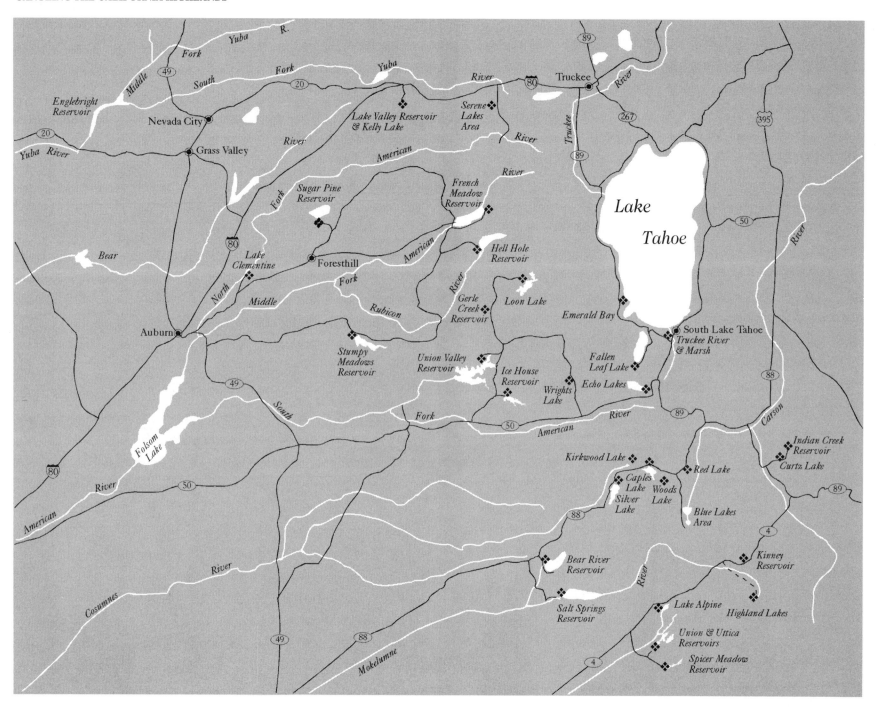

The Tahoe Sierra

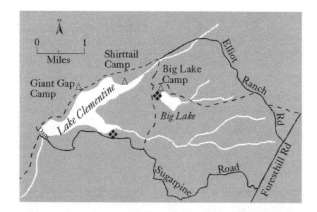

Sugar Pine Reservoir & Big Lake

Description   This small serene lake is nestled among the pines and evergreens at 3,618 feet elevation. The lake has 160 surface acres and several coves and inlets to expolore. When the lake is still the shoreline reflections are captivating. The is a 10 mph speed limit on the lake so power boats are not a problem. Nearby Big Lake makes a nice side trip.

Camping   All these campgrounds have piped water, toilets, tables and fireplaces for a fee: Shirttail, 30 sites, reservations through Destinet: 800-444-7275 - Giant Gap, 30 sites, reservations through Destinet: 800-444-7275 - Big Lake, 120 sites, reservations thru Big Lake Resort: 530-367-2129.

Directions   From Interstate 80 at Auburn take the Foresthill exit, go east on Foresthill Road about 8 miles past the town of Foresthill to Sugar Pine Road, go north on Sugar Pine Road to the lake and campgrounds.

Resources   Tahoe National Forest Map from USFS, Dutch Hill topo map from USGS, brochure from Foresthill Ranger Station (see information below).

Advisory   Big Lake and all campgrounds are closed November through April.

Information   Foresthill Ranger Station: 530-367-2224

Clouds paint pictures above Sugar Pine Reservoir

Water spirits reflected in Sugar Pine Reservoir

Lake Clementine

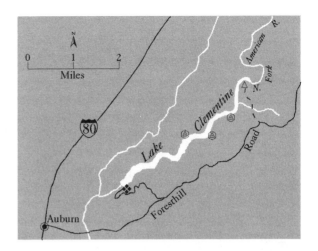

Description   Lake Clementine is a beautiful lake which offers both long distance paddling and paddle-in camping opportunities. It rests in the pine and fir trees of the Sierra foothills at 3,618 feet along the North Fork American River. It is a long thin body of water about 3 and a half miles long with 160 surface acres. At it's widest the lake is less than 200 yards wide and upstream less than 200 feet wide. This makes Lake Clementine very intimate and really enhances the sense of being an explorer on a river. The upper end is very shallow and devoid of power boats. As you paddle upstream you can see the bottom of the lake slip by in the shallower water. The last half mile of upstream paddling is pretty strenuous as the lake becomes the flow of the North Fork American River (so that's what it feels like to be a salmon). The dam is an over-the-top spillway and the lake stays filled year round.

Camping   There are 3 boat-in camps along the shores of the lake with toilets and fire rings but no water, no fees, no reservations.

Directions   From Interstate 80 at Auburn take the Foresthill exit and go south on Foresthill Road about 3.5 miles to the Lake Clementine turnoff to the left, go about 2.5 to parking and the boat ramp.

Resources   Auburn & Greenwood topo maps from USGS.

Advisory   Watch for power boats. Bring your own water or a water filter.

Information   Auburn State Recreation Area: 530-885-4527.

Lake Clementine's twists and turns

End of the line as the American River enters Lake Clementine

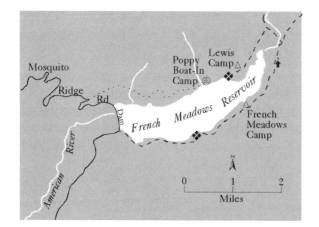

French Meadows Reservoir

Description French Meadow Reservoir is a pretty mountain lake with deep blue water. It offers a good long paddle end to end and has a boat-in campground. It sits at 5,200 feet elevation with 1,920 surface acres when full. In dry years this lake is subject to severe drawdowns in late summer, leaving it little more than a puddle with a bad case of reservoir ring. You should call ahead to check water levels. Waterskiing and jet ski can be plentiful on French Meadows Reservoir even though they are discouraged due to the many submerged hazards leaving the lake to paddlers and fishermen.

Camping These campgrounds have tables, fireplaces, and toilets for a fee: French Meadows, 75 sites, piped water, flush toilets, reservations through Destinet: 800-444-7275 - Ahart, no water, no reservations - Lewis, 40 sites, piped water, reservations through Destinet: 800-444-7275 - Poppy, 12 paddle-in sites, no water, no fees or reservations.

Directions From Interstate 80 just east of Auburn take the Foresthill exit, go east on Foresthill Road about 15 miles to the town of Foresthill; from Foresthill take Mosquito Ridge Road (a truly long and winding road) east for about 35 miles to the reservoir and campgrounds.

Resources Tahoe National Forest map from USFS; Bunker Hill and Royal Gorge topo maps from USGS.

Advisory If thunderstorms come up, get off the water! Watch for power boats. Bring your own water to the boat-in camp. Keep an eye out for bears. They're fun to watch but don't let them get at your food. Extreme seasonal changes in reservoir level. Afternoon winds can get strong enough to be dangerous. Winter snows make the lake inaccessible.

Information Tahoe National Forest: 530-367-2224

Alpine thunderheads reflect in French Meadow Reservoir

Hell Hole Reservoir

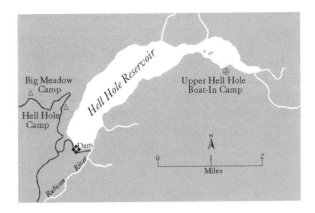

Description   Hell Hole Reservoir is a gorgeous paddling spot, especially at it's eastern end. There are plenty of islands to explore and beautiful mountain vistas. It rests at 4,700 ft in the granite bound gorge of the Rubicon River. At peak levels this alpine reservoir has 1,300 acres of clear, winter-cold water that has a deep blue hue. Open May-October.

Camping   All these campgrounds have tables, fireplaces, and toilets: Upper Hell Hole boat-incamp, 15 sites, no water, no fees, noreservations - Hell Hole, 10 sites, piped water, fee, no reservations - Big Meadow, 55 sites, piped water, flush toilets, fee, reservations through Destinet: 800-444-7275.

Directions   From Interstate 80 at Auburn take the Foresthill exit and go east on Foresthill Road to the town of Foresthill, from there go east on Mosquito Ridge Road to French Meadows Road to the south end of French Meadows Reservoir, go south on Forest Service Road 48 (gravel road) to Hell Hole Reservoir.There is a parking lot and a boat ramp at the dam.

Resources   Tahoe National Forest map from USFS, Bunker Hill and Wentworth Springs topo maps from USGS.

The Rubicon River feeds Hell Hole Reservoir

Advisory   If thunderstorms come up, get off the water! Watch for power boats. Bring your own water to the boat-in camp. Keep an eye out for bears. They're fun to watch but don't let them get at your food. Extreme seasonal changes in reservoir level. Afternoon winds can get strong enough to be dangerous. Winter snows make the lake inaccessible.

Information   Placer County Water Agency: 530-367-2291

Doesn't look like a Hell Hole to me

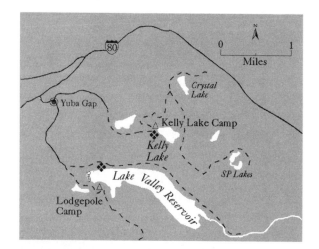

Lake Valley Reservoir & Kelly Lake

Description   These two mountain lakes sit next to each other in the conifer forests of the Sierra at about 5,800 feet elevation. With easy access of Interstate 80 and power boating restriction on both lakes, this is a quiet paddling getaway to the Sierra Nevada.

Lake Valley Reservoir has 300 surface acres offering a nice long distance paddle. Power boating is prohibited on Lake Valley and the little fishing motor boats don't pose much of a wake threat.

Kelly Lake is a very small, pretty lake that is perfect for a quiet float. Motors of any kind are prohibited on Kelly Lake. This lake gets little use and you will often find yourself alone to float peacefully with only the wind and birdsongs to disturb perfect quiet.

Camping   Lodgepole Campground on Lake Valley Reservoir has 18 sites with running water, toilets, tables and fireplaces for a fee, no reservations.

Directions   From Interstate 80 take the Yuba Gap exit and go south, turn right on Lake Valley Road to the lake and campground.

Resources   Tahoe National Forest map from USFS; Cisco Grove topo map from USGS.

Advisory   On Lake Valley Reservoir steady west winds can get a bit overwhelming for the canoeist, especially in the afternoon. If thunderstorms come up, get off the water!

Information   PG&E Regional Land Department: 800-552-4743 or 530-529-6316

Lake Valley Reservoir

Small and quiet Kelly Lake

Serene Lakes Area

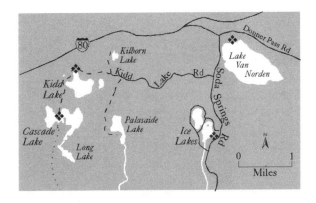

Description   These small lakes off Interstate 80 offer some quiet boating on waters where motors are not allowed. They rest at about 6,500 feet elevation among the granite boulders and pine forests of the Tahoe National Forest. They say there is a boat ramp for Kidd Lake, I never found it. Cascade Lake can be hard to reach if the road is in poor shape, but it is a wonderful paddling lake. The shores of Ice Lakes are developed with houses, but it is still a pretty mellow place. I'm not sure if it's really okay to canoe on Lake Van Norden. When I was there I didn't see any "no trespassing" signs and I had a wonderful time paddling around. I never did find anyone to say "yay" or "nay", so I guess you paddle Van Norden Lake at your own risk.

Camping   The nearest individual camping is at Lake Valley Reservoir (*see previous page*).

Directions   All lakes: from Interstate 80 about 12 miles west of Truckee take the Norden exit, go south on Soda Springs Road. For Ice Lakes go south on Soda Springs Road for about 2 miles, the lakes are on the west side of the road. For Kidd Lake, go south on Soda Springs Road for about 1 mile, go west on Kidd Lake Road for another mile, veer south where the road forks to Kidd Lake. For Cascade Lake, continue on Kidd Lake Road past Kidd Lake to Cascade Lake, the road beyond Kidd Lake is rough and sometimes washed out. For Lake Van Norden, park on the shoulder of the road at the corner of Soda Springs Road and Donner Pass Road, then portage your canoe over the Van Norden dam.

Kidd Lake

Resources   Tahoe National Forest map from USFS, Soda Springs topo map from USGS.

Advisory   Heavy snows blanket the area from as early as October to as late as June. Bring your own water.

Information   Tahoe National Forest: 530-587-3558, Pacific Gas & Electric: 530-386-5164, Serene Lakes Lodge: 530-426-9001

Ice Lakes

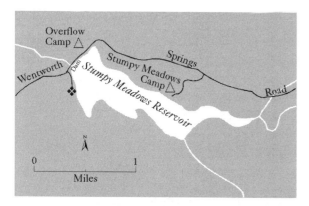

Stumpy Meadows Reservoir

Description   Stumpy Meadows Reservoir is a beautiful lake sitting at 4,260 feet evelation among the pine trees including some huge ponderosa pines. The 320 surface acres of clear, cold water has a 5mph speed limit. Swimming is an exhilarating experience at Stumpy Meadows. The lake is open from April through November, weather permitting.

Camping   Stumpy Meadows Campground has 40 sites with piped water water, toilets, tables and fireplaces for a fee, reservations through Destinet: 800-444-7275.

Directions   From Intersate 5 at Auburn take Hwy 49 south to the junction of Hwy 193 in the town of Cool, go east on Hwy 193 to Georgetown, go east on Wentworth Springs Road to the lake and campgrounds.

Resources   El Dorado National Forest Map from USFS, Devil Peak topo map from USGS.

Advisory   Lake and campgrounds are closed from December through March. Winter snows make the area inaccessible.

Information   Georgetown Ranger District: 530-333-4312.

Stumpy Meadows Reservoir

Ice House Reservoir

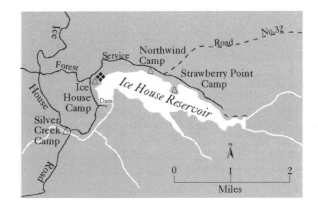

Description Ice House Reservoir rests nestled in the granite peaks of the Crystal Range in the El Dorado National Forest at 5,500 feet elevation with 678 surface acres. Ice House Reservoir is a man-made lake filled with clear sierra-snow melt water. Open June through October.

Camping Ice House campground has 83 sites (17 for tent only), with piped water, toilets, tables and fireplaces for a fee, no reservations. Northwind campground has 10 sites with toilets, tables and fireplaces but no water, no fees or reservations. Strawberry Point has toilets, tables and fireplaces but no water, no fees or reservations.

Directions From Sacramento take Hwy 50 about 10 miles past the town of Pollock Pines to the town of Riverton, at Riverton go north on Ice House Road about 11 miles to the sign for Ice House Reservoir, go east on Ice House Reservoir access road about 1 mile to the lake and campgrounds.

Resources El Dorado National Forest map from USFS, Kyburz topo map from USGS.

Advisory Watch for power boats and afternoon winds. Winter snows make the area inaccessible. Bring your own water.

Information Pacific Ranger District: 530-644-2349

Looking south over Ice House Reservoir

Looking east over Ice House Reservoir

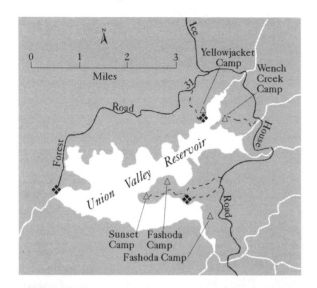

Union Valley Reservoir

Description   Union Valley Reservoir rests at 4,900 feet with 2,860 surface acres. Because of it's setting among pine and fir forests and the granite peaks of the Crystal Range this is a very pretty lake and quite popular, especially on summer weekends. Union Valley is a big lake with some good paddle-in camping and long distance paddling opportunities. The lake is open from June through October.

Camping   All these campground have tables, fireplaces and toilets: Jones Fork, 10 sites, no water, no fees, nreservations - Fashoda, 30 paddle-in sites, no water, no fees no reservations - Sunset, 131 sites, piped water, toilets, camp fee, no reservations - Wench Creek, 100 sites, piped water, flush toilets, camp fee, reservations through Destinet: 800-444-7275 - Yellowjacket, 40 sites, piped water, camp fee, reservations through Destinet: 800-444-7275.

Directions   From Sacramento take Hwy 50 about 10 miles past the town of Pollock Pines to the town of Riverton, at Riverton go north on Ice House Road about 15 miles to the lake and campgrounds. Union Valley Reservoir is visible from Ice House Road past Ice House Reservoir.

Resources   El Dorado National Forest map from USFS; Robbs Peak, Loon Lake, Riverton and Kyburz topo maps from USGS.

Advisory   Watch for power boats and afternoon winds. Bring your own water or a water filter for the paddle-in camp. Closed in winter.

Information   Pacific Ranger District: 530-644-2349

Union Valley Reservoir

Union Valley Reservoir

Wrights Lake

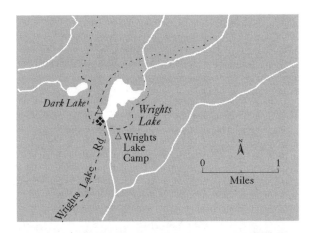

Description Wrights Lake is a natural lake nestled in the high mountains at 7,000 feet elevation. Motors of any kind are prohibited on this 65 acre lake which assures you of a nice quiet paddle. Although it's mighty cold, you can swim in the snow melt waters of Wrights Lake or take advantage of the many granite bound trails in the area. The lake is open from June through October.

Camping Wrights Lake campground has 71 sites,(35 for tent only), with running water, flush toilets, tables, fireplaces and showers for a fee, reservations through Destinet: 800-444-7275. Camping along the shoreline is allowed as long as you get a fire permit from the ranger station in Pollock Pines.

Directions From Sacramento take Hwy 50 about 5 miles east of Kyburz to Wrights Lake road, go north on Wrights Lake Road about 8 miles to the lake and campground. When I went to Wrights Lake, Wright Lake Road was closed due to heavy rain erosion. Call ahead to check road conditions and check for alternate routes.

Resources El Dorado National Forest map from USFS, Pyramid Peak topo map from USGS.

Advisory Winter snows make the area inaccessible.

Information Pacific Ranger District: 530-644-2349

Wrights Lake   *Courtesy U.S. Forest Service*

Residences on Wrights Lake   *Courtesy U.S. Forest Service*

Loon Lake

Islands abound on Loon Lake

Tiny and pretty Gerle Creek Reservoir

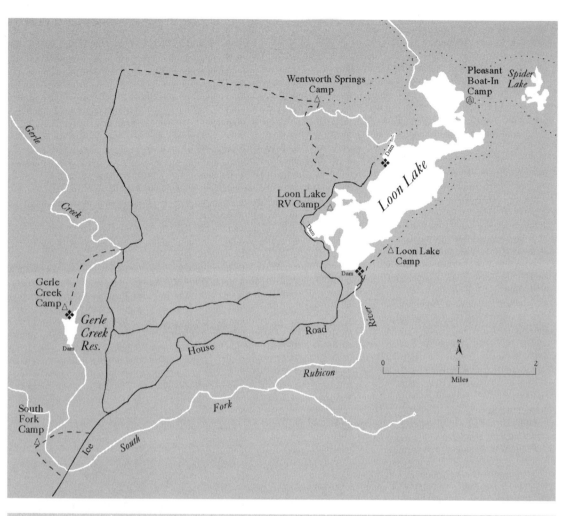

The wide view of Loon Lake

Loon Lake & Gerle Creek Reservoir

Description   Loon Lake is a high mountain lake sitting at 6,500 ft. near the western edge of Desolation Wilderness. This is a gorgeous lake with a granite shoreline and many islands to paddle around and explore. One of the highlights of this lake is a boat-in camp at the north end of the lake which affords a chance to do some paddle-in camping. You can also get in quite a few strokes paddling end to end. Water skiing and jet skis are allowed even though the water is frigid, so watch for boats. The lake is surrounded by mountains and the atmosphere is truly majestic. There are many trails to explore including a short hike to beautiful Spider Lake or an extended backpacking trip into Desolation Wilderness. You could backpack to Emerald Bay or D.L.Bliss State Park on Lake Tahoe.

Camping   Pleasant boat-in camp has 10 campsites with toilets, tables and fireplaces, but no water, no fees, no reservations - Loon Lake campground has 53 campsites with water, toilets, tables and fireplaces for a fee, reservations through Destinet: 800-444-7275 - Northshore RV has 15 campsites with toilets, tables and fireplaces, no fees, no reservations.

Directions   From Hwy 50 at Riverton, take Ice House Road north 32 miles, the road ends at Loon Lake.

Resources   El Dorado National Forest map from USFS, Wentworth Springs and Loon Lake topo maps from USGS.

Advisory   Bring your own water. Even though waterskiing is not advised, watch for power boats anyway.

Information   Pacific Ranger Station: 530-644-2348

Quiet, intimate beauty on Gerle Creek Reservoir

Many granite islands dot Loon Lake

Sunrise on Loon Lake

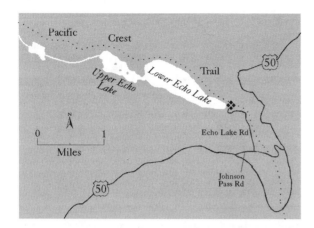

Echo Lakes have beautiful, clear, blue water

Lower Echo Lake from the Pacific Crest Trail

Echo Lakes

Description

Echo Lakes are actually one lake with a skinny passage between the two sections. They rest at 7,500 feet elevation at the crest of the Sierra Nevada near Echo Summit. This is a truly gorgeous, alpine lake. It's a little commercialized for my tastes, but once you get on the water, it's pretty nice. Water skiing is prohibited on Upper Echo Lake providing the best quiet paddling here. However, you have to paddle the length of Lower Echo Lake to get to Upper Echo Lake. While you're on the lower lake, stay near shore to avoid power boats.

Since there is no camping available at Echo Lakes, it is best paddled as a side trip rather than a canoeing/camping destination. There is a beautiful trail that leads from the dam to the west shore of Upper Echo Lake and beyond into Desolation Wilderness. Check out the view of the Lake Tahoe Basin off the hiking trail east of the dam.

Camping

There is a rather expensive lodge at Echo Lakes that requires reservations. The nearest campgrounds are back along Hwy 50 or down around Lake Tahoe.

Directions

From Sacramento take Hwy 50 east to Johnson Pass Road just before the summit (when I was there the sign for Echo Lakes was missing), go north on Johnson Pass Road to left on Echo Lakes Road, go about 1 mile to the lake. Drop your canoe off down at the bottom parking lot, if the bottom lot is full, drive back up to the top parking lot. Parking can be hard to come by. There is a $6.00 put-in fee, payable at the dock house.

Resources

El Dorado National Forest map from USFS, Echo Lake topo map from USGS.

Advisory

Watch for power boats on Lower Echo Lake. Bring your own water. There is no camping at Echo Lakes.

Information

Lake Tahoe Basin Management Unit: 530-573-2600 or Echo Chalet: 530-659-7207

Fallen Leaf Lake

Description   Fallen Leaf Lake is Lake Tahoe's little sister. Its water is the same crystal clear, deep blue with turquoise shallows. It's three miles long and a little less than one mile wide and sits at 6,400 feet just south of Lake Tahoe with mountain peaks and forests rising up from the shoreline. Fallen Leaf is surrounded by privately owned houses, but it still has spectacular beauty in abundance. Jet skiing is prohibited, but water skiing is allowed.

Camping   Fallen Leaf campground has 205 sites (75 for tents only) with piped water, tables, fireplaces and flush toilets for a fee, reservations through Destinet: 800-444-7275.

Directions   Whether you're coming to Lake Tahoe on Interstate 80 or Hwy 50, Fallen Leaf Lake Road is off Hwy 89, three miles west of the town of South Lake Tahoe, Fallen Leaf Lake Road turns into a one lane road when it gets near the lake. Drive slow and be courteous with traffic. Remember you have a canoe on top of your car and you represent all other canoeists.

Resources   El Dorado National Forest map from USFS, Emerald Bay topo map from USGS.

Advisory   Watch for power boats. Afternoon winds can get very strong. Respect the privacy of the land owners around the lake. Winter snows make the lake and campground inaccessible.

Information   Lake Tahoe Basin Management Unit: 530-573-2600, Fallen Leaf Lake Marina: 530-544-0787

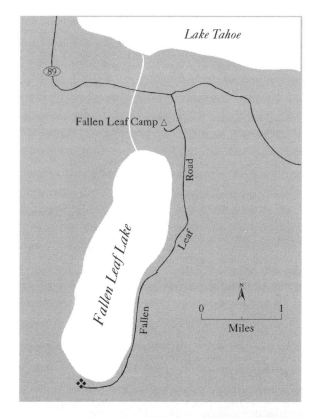

The clear, turquoise waters of Fallen Leaf Lake

Eagle Falls near Emerald Bay

Waterfowl feeding in Truckee Marsh

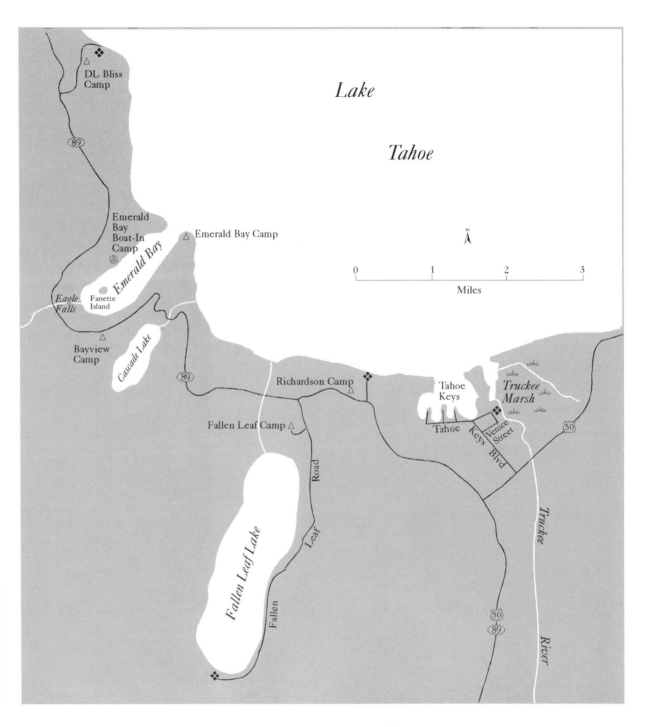

Lake

Tahoe

DL Bliss
Camp

89

Emerald
Bay
Boat-In
Camp

Emerald Bay Camp

Emerald Bay

*Eagle
Falls*

Fanette
Island

Bayview
Camp

Cascade Lake

89

Richardson Camp

Fallen Leaf Camp

Tahoe
Keys

Tahoe

Keys Blvd

Venice
Street

*Truckee
Marsh*

50

Fallen Leaf Lake

Leaf
Road

Fallen

50
89

*Truckee
River*

N

0   1   2   3

Miles

Still reflective morning on Emerald Bay

Lake Tahoe Area

Description Lake Tahoe rests among the forested granite peaks of the Sierra Nevada at 6,300 feet elevation.

Emerald Bay is a natural feature of Lake Tahoe. There are so many unique features at Emerald Bay (paddle-in camping, a tea house on Fannette Island, Vikingsholm, Eagle Falls, Rubicon trail and the Tahoe Queen paddle wheel boat) it's like a little theme park. Paddling into Emerald Bay's boat-in camp from D.L.Bliss State Park, spending the night, exploring Emerald Bay's many treasures and paddling back to D.L.Bliss is one of the great canoe adventures available in California. Fallen Leaf Lake, Lake Tahoe's little sister is a nice, nearby side trip.

The Truckee River is one of the best unknown paddling destinations in California. From the put-in near the yacht harbor you can go down stream to the gorgeous Truckee Marsh where the Truckee River enters southern Lake Tahoe. This is not to be confused with the Truckee River that flows out of northern Lake Tahoe and flows to Reno.

Camping All these campgrounds have piped water, tables, fireplaces and toilets for a fee: Emerald Bay, 20 boat-in sites, no reservations - D.L.Bliss State Park, 168 sites, flush toilets, showers, reservations through Destinet: 800-444-7275 - Fallen Leaf Lake, 205 sites, flush toilets, reservations at 800-280-2267 - Camp Richardson Resort, 223 sites, flush toilets, hot showers, laundromat, reservations at 800-544-1801.

Directions For all destinations: from Sacramento take Hwy 50 to the junction with Hwy 89 at South Lake Tahoe. For Fallen Leaf Lake and Emerald Bay: follow the map to the destinations and campgrounds. All roads are clearly marked. For Truckee River and Truckee Marsh: from Hwy 50 in South Lake Tahoe go north on Harbor Blvd. to ??? Way, follow ??? Way to the entrance to the Yatch Harbor. Park before the entrance next to the Truckee River and put-in there.

Resources Emerald Bay USGS topo map; Tahoe National map from USFS.

Advisory Boat wakes and wind waves make the open wates of Lake Tahoe unsafe for open canoes. The water is always cold and hypothermia is a definite danger if you capsize. Stay near shore. Always wear your PFD.

Information USFS Tahoe Basin Management Unit: 530-573-2600, Emerald Bay State Park: 530-541-3030, D.L.Bliss State Park: 530-525-7277

Sunrise on Emerald Bay

The Truckee River meanders toward Lake Tahoe

The Truckee River enters southern Lake Tahoe at the Truckee Marsh

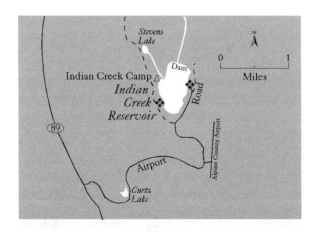

Indian Creek Reservoir

Description	Indian Creek Reservoir sits on the eastern side of the Sierra Nevada at 5,600 feet elevation among Jeffrey and pinon pines with the granite crest of the Sierras off to the west and the high Nevada desert off to the east. Its 160 surface acres of water make a wonderful, quiet paddle amidst beautiful scenery. Water skiing and jet skis are prohibited. The winds can be quite fierce as they swoosh down from the Sierra summit.
	On the way into Indian Creek you pass Curtz Lake (pond). Although this is a tiny lake, it does offer a pleasant little float in a gorgeous setting. Don't use your paddle too much, you run out of lake quickly.
Camping	Indian Creek Camp has 29 sites with tables, fireplaces, toilets and piped water for a fee, no reservations.
Directions	From the Hwy 89/50 junction at South Lake Tahoe go south on Hwy 89 through the junction with Hwy 88, stay on Hwy 89 south at the 89/88 split at the town of Woodsford, continue south on Hwy 89 to the Indian Springs Reservoir sign, go east on the Indian Creek Reservoir access road (Airport Road) 8 miles to the reservoir. You pass by Curtz Lake on the way.
Resources	Toiyabe National Forest/Carson Ranger District map from USFS, Markleeville topo map from USGS.
Advisory	Winds can be fierce. Bring your own water.
Information	Bureau of Land Management: 702-885-6100.

The east edge of the Sierras overlook Indian Creek Reservoir

Tiny Curtz Lake

Bear River & Salt Springs Reservoirs

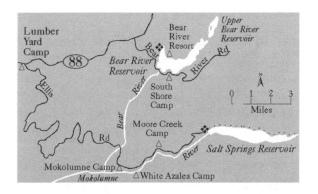

Description Salt Springs Reservoir sits at 3,900 feet elevation in the deep granite gorge of the Mokelumne River. Don't be lookin' to get out of your canoe anywhere between the boat ramp and the very east end of the lake, the canyon walls are just too steep. The feeling at Salt Springs Reservoir is awesome and daunting. If you paddle this lake, do so in the early morning. By noon the winds start to come up the canyon and by afternoon they can really howl, raising white caps and making the trip back to the boat ramp can be a little too adventurous. Only hand launched boats can get to the boat ramp over the dam.

Bear River Reservoir has a friendly feel, but it's quite a bit more developed and crowded. The lake rests at 5,800 feet elevation with 546 surface acres. Power boats and jet skis abound in the summer months at this popular resort lake. The eastern end of Bear River Reservoir is very pretty.

Camping These campgrounds on Bear River Reservoir have tables, fireplaces, toilets and piped water for a fee: South Shore, 22 sites (13 for tent only, 4 two-family sites), no reservations - Bear River Resort, 127 sites, flush toilets, showers, store, laundromat, phone, etc., reservations advised at 209-295-4868. Along the Mokelumne River near Salt Springs Reservoir all these campgrounds have tables, fireplaces and toilets, but no water, no fee, no reservations: Mokelumne, 8 sites for tent only - Moore Creek, 8 sites for tent only - White Azalea, 6 sites for tent only. Bring your own water to these campgrounds.

Bear River Reservoir

Directions For Salt Springs Reservoir: from Hwy 99 in Stockton take Hwy 88 east about 70 miles into the mountains to Ellis Road (its easy to pass by this turnoff, the only marking being a sign for Lumber Yard Campground), go south on Ellis Road (Forest Service Road 92) about 8 miles, cross the Bear River and keep an eye out for Forest Service Road 9, take Forest Service Road 9 to the campgrounds and the lake beyond. For Bear River Reservoir: continue on past the Lumber Yard turnoff about 10 more miles to the Bear River Reservoir turnoff, go south on Bear River Road to the lake and campgrounds.

Resources El Dorado National Forest map from USFS - Peddler Hill, Bear River Reservoir and Calaveras Dome topo maps from USGS.

Advisory Watch for power boats on Bear River Reservoir. The afternoonwinds can be very strong, especially on Salt Springs Reservoir. Bring your own water to Salt Springs Reservoir.

Information El Dorado National Forest: 209-295-4251, Bear River Resort: 209-295-4868.

Salt Springs Reservoir sits in its granite gorge

Idyllic, natural Woods Lake

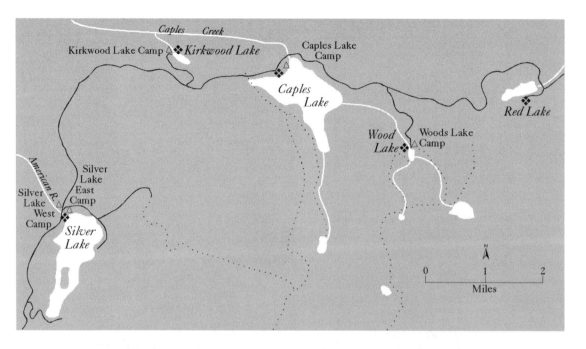

Sierra peaks loom over Caples Lake

Red Lake from Carson Pass

Silver Lake

Carson Pass Area

Description   This group of lakes along Hwy 88 (the Carson Pass National Scenic Byway) in the high mountains make a wonderful canoeing vacation. All these lakes are incredibly scenic and afford the canoeist one of the most pleasant paddling experiences of anywhere in California. Granite peaks and forested shorelines are everywhere and the waters are clear and cold.

Silver Lake sits at 7,200 feet elevation with a good sized island in the middle. Water skiing and jet skis are allowed on Silver Lake. Kirkwood Lake is a small, natural, quiet lake which rests at 7,600 feet elevation and prohibits motors of any kind. Caples Lake has 600 surface acres at 7,950 feet elevation and has a 5mph speed limit. Woods Lake is a truly beautiful, natural lake and is the highest of the lakes at 8,200 feet elevation. Motors of any kind are prohibited on Woods Lake. Red Lake is an undeveloped lake at about 8,000 feet elevation with all motors prohibited. All the lakes close due to winter and spring snows.

Camping   All these campgrounds have piped water, tables, fireplaces and toilets for a fee: Silver LakeWest, 17 sites, no reservations - Silver Lake East, 62 sites (28 for tent only), no reservations - Kirkwood Lake, 12 sites for tents only with water, no reservations - Caples Lake, 35 sites (20 for tent only), reservations through 800-280-2267 - Woods Lake, 25 sites for tent only, no reservations. Red Lake has some undeveloped sites with fireplaces, no water, no toilets, no fees, no reservations.

Directions   For Silver Lake: from Hwy 99 in Stockton take Hwy 88 east about 90 miles into the mountains to the lake and campgrounds. For Kirkwood Lake: continue on Hwy 88 past Silver Lake about 4 miles to the Kirkwood Lake turnoff, go north on the access road to the lake and campground. For Caples Lake: continue on Hwy 88 past Kirkwood Lake just a few miles, Caples Lake and the campground are right next to the highway. For Woods Lake: continue on Hwy 88 past Caples Lake and turn south off Hwy 88 when you see the sign for Woods Lake, it's less than a mile to the lake and campground. Red Lake sits right on Hwy 88 about 1.5 miles east of Carson Pass.

Resources   El Dorado National Forest map from USFS, Caples Lake and Carson Pass topo maps from USGS.

Advisory   Winter snows make this area inaccessible. Watch for power boats on Silver Lake.

Information   El Dorado National Forest: 530-644-6048.

Caples Lake

The marshy end of Silver Lake

Kirkwood Lake

Looking southeast across Tamarack Lake

Mountain vistas behind Upper Blue Lake

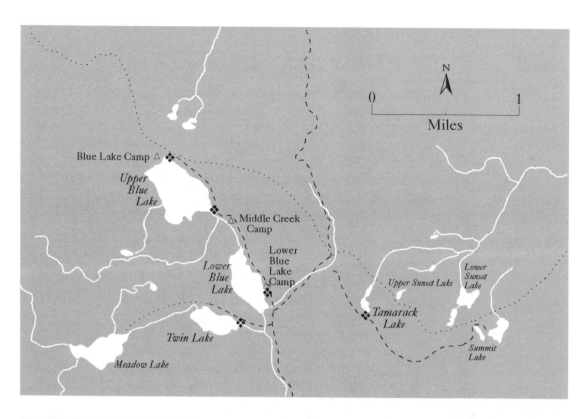

Twin Lake

Morning at Lower Blue Lake

Blue Lakes Area

Description   The Blue Lakes area sits just east of the Carson Pass at about 8,000 feet elevation. There are five gorgeous lakes in the area on which to paddle. All lakes have pristine, alpine scenery and will surely transport you to paddler's paradise. Power boats and jet skis are prohibited on all these lakes.

Upper Blue Lake sits at 8,136 feet and is the largest of the three with wide mountain vistas. Lower Blue Lake sits at 8,050 feet with several islands and the inlet of Middle Creek to explore. Twin Lake is a narrow lake that sits at 8,142 feet and is surrounded by pines and granite boulders. Tamarack Lake is a tiny lake with a beautiful shoreline. For a great view, paddle to the north shore of Tamarack Lake, opposite the dam and hike to the top of the hill there. For a short hike it's spectacular. If you have a 4 wheel drive vehicle you can also explore paddling on tiny Upper and Lower Sunset Lakes to the east. The Mokelumne Wilderness is right next to Blue Lakes with many miles of hiking and backpacking adventure. The Pacific Crest Trail runs nearby. The lakes are inaccessible until late spring and close again around the end of October.

Camping   All these campground have piped water, tables, fireplaces and toilets for a fee, no reservations: Lower Blue Lake, 16 sites for tents only - Middle Creek, 5 sites - Upper Blue Lake Dam, 25 sites for tents only - Upper Blue Lake, 32 sites for tents only.

Directions   From South Lake Tahoe take Hwy 89 south over Luther Pass to the junction with Hwy 88, go west on Hwy 88 turn south on Blue Lakes Road and drive 12 miles (7 miles paved, 5 miles gravel) to the lakes and campgrounds.

Resources   El Dorado National Forest map from USFS, Carson Pass and Pacific Valley topo maps from USGS.

Advisory   Winter snows make the area inaccessible.

Information   Toiyabe National Forest: 702-882-2766 or Pacific Gas & Electric: 800-743-5000

Middle Creek enters Lower Blue Lake

Upper Blue Lake

Small, intimate Tamarack Lake

Uttica Reservoir

Nearby Mosquito Lakes provide a very pretty alpine float

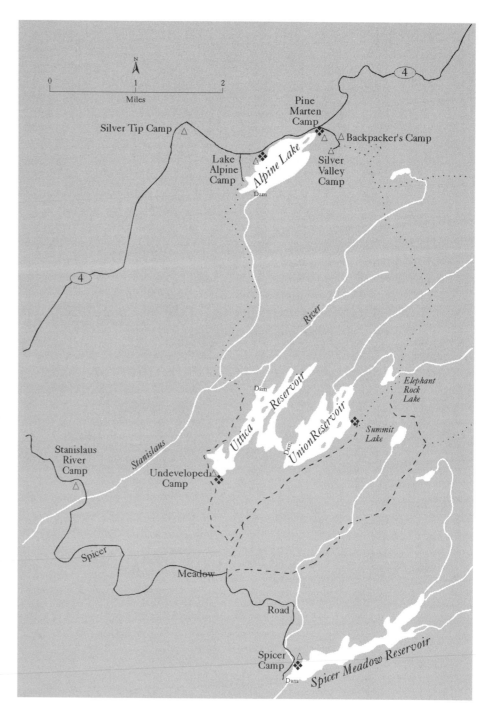

Lake Alpine/Spicer, Union & Utica Reservoirs

Description   This high mountain area along the Stanislaus River in Bear Valley makes for a great paddling vacation. All these island dotted, high mountain lakes sit nestled among the granite peaks of the Sierra Nevada. Water skiing and jet skis are prohibited on all the lakes making this a haven for paddlers.

Spicer Meadow Reservoir sits at 6,418 feet elevation. At 277 surface acres, Spicer Meadow is the biggest of these lakes and provides the long distance paddling for the area.

Utica and Union Reservoirs sit right next to each other at 6,850 feet elevation. Both these lakes allow dispersed lakeside camping as long as you follow the rules posted on the bulletin boards. So, paddle out, find a spot and set up camp.

Lake Alpine sits at 7,320 feet elevation with 180 surface acres. This is the most developed of these lakes and the place is often packed in the summer months. There is a strictly enforced 10 m.p.h. speed limit on the lake (try not to paddle to fast, wouldn't want to get a ticket).

This area truly deserves the title of "Paddler's Paradise". It's so pretty here, you'll have to pinch yourself to make sure you're not dreaming.

Camping   All these campgrounds have tables, fireplaces, toilets and piped water for a fee, no reservations: Stanislaus River, 25 sites - Spicer Meadow, 60 sites - Silver Tip, 24 sites, flush toilets - Lake Alpine, 5 sites, flush toilets, showers - Pine Marten, 33 sites, flush toilets - Silver Valley, 25 sites, flush toilets. Utica and Union Reservoirs allow dispersed camping, follow the posted rules of etiquette.

Directions   For Spicer Meadow, Utica and Union Reservoirs: take Hwy 49 to the town of Angels Camp, go east on Hwy 4 about 32 miles, go southeast on Spicer Meadow Road (Rd. 7N01), follow the signs to the lakes and campgrounds. For Lake Alpine: continue east on Hwy 4 about 3 miles past the town of Bear Valley, the lake is right next to the road on the south side.

Resources   Stanislaus National Forest map from USFS, Tamarack and Spicer Meadow topo maps from USGS.

Advisory   Afternoon winds can be very strong, especially on Spicer Meadow Reservoir. Winter snows make this area inaccessible. Bring your own water.

Information   Stanislaus National Forest: 209-795-1381, Lake Alpine Resort: 209-753-6358

Spicer Meadow Reservoir

Alpine Lake

Union Reservoir

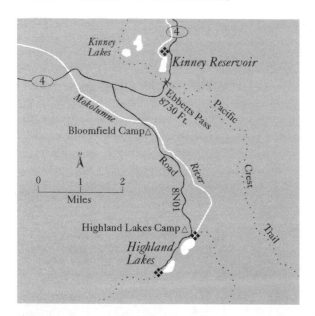

Highland Lakes & Kinney Reservoir

Description   All three of these lakes sit high in the Sierra Nevada near Ebbetts Pass. Upper and Lower Highland Lakes are very small natural lakes that sit at 8,600 feet elevation. They are surrounded by mountain peaks including Hiram Peak which sits right behind Highland Lakes at 9,760 feet elevation. The first of Highland Lakes drains to the north and is actually the headwaters of the Mokolumne River. Though they are really no more than ponds, Highland Lakes make for a very pleasant float in some rarified alpine air.

Kinney Reservoir sits at about 9,000 feet elevation in an idyllic alpine setting. Surrounded by mountain crags, this small lake sits in a granite bowl and gets almost no boat traffic.

Camping   Highland Lakes camp has 35 sites with piped water, tables, fireplaces and toilets for a fee, no reservations. Bloomfield camp has 5 sites with tables, fireplaces and toilets, but no water, no fee, no reservations.

Directions   For Highland Lakes: take Hwy 49 to the town of Angels Camp, go east on Hwy 4 to Lake Alpine, continue on Hwy 4 past Lake Alpine about 15 miles, keep an eye out for the Highland Lakes sign (it's kind of a small sign), go southeast on Highland Lakes Road (Forest Service Road 8N01) and drive about 8 miles to the lakes and campground. For Kinney Reservoir: at the Highland Lakes turnoff continue east of Hwy 88 about 1 mile past Ebbetts Pass, the lake is on the west side of the road, put in at the dam.

Resources   Stanislaus National Forest map from USFS, Ebbetts Pass and Dardenelles Cone topo maps from USGS

Advisory   Winter snows makes this area inaccessible. Bring your own water.

Information   Stanislaus National Forest: 209-795-1381

Hiram Peak rises behind Highland Lakes

Kinney Reservoir sits in it's bowl

Lake Alpine

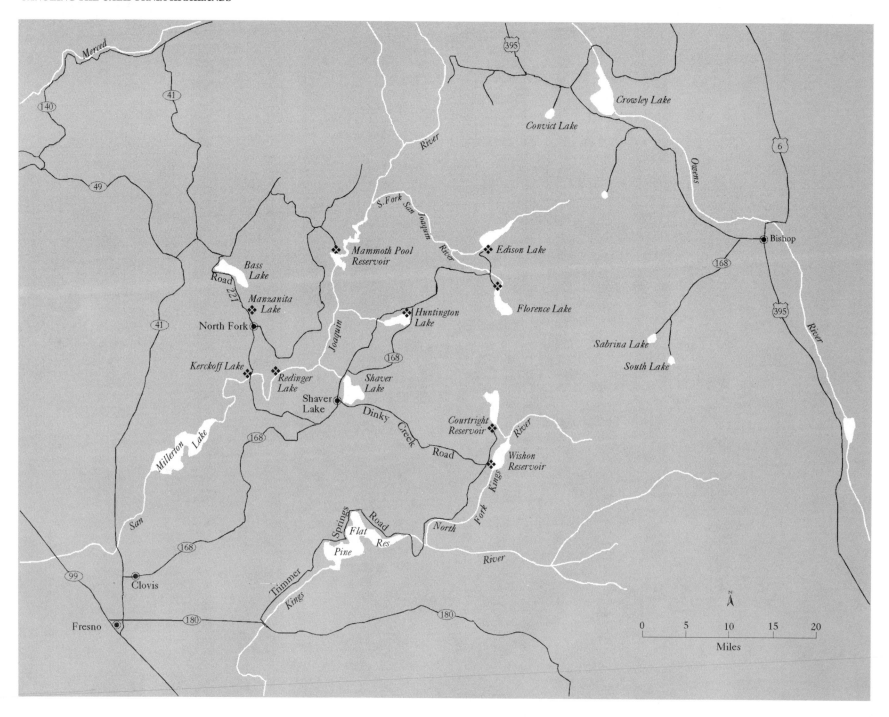

The Southwest Sierra

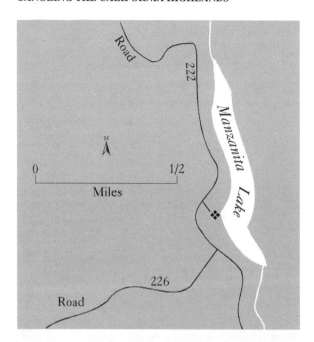

Manzanita Lake

Description   This is one of those places that nobody has ever heard of, including the people who are already there. Manzanita Lake is a tiny little fishing lake that I found completely charming for canoeing. It is less than 1 mile long and only a stone's throw across, but paddling upstream among the water grasses upstream is a most pleasant exploration.

Camping   See Kerckoff Lake, "Camping", next page.

Directions   From Hwy 99 in Madera take Hwy 145 east to Hwy 41, take Hwy 41 north about 25 miles to County Road 200 (North Fork Road), go east and north to the town of North Fork, from North Fork go north on County Road 222 to Manzanita Lake on the east side of the road

Resources   Sierra National Forest map from USFS, Bass Lake and North Fork topo maps from USGS.

Advisory   Have as much fun as possible.

Information   Sierra National Forest: 209-683-4665

Idyllic canoeing upstream on Manzanita Lake

Kerckoff Lake

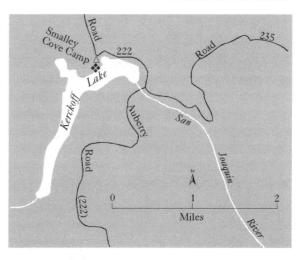

Description   Kerckoff Lake is a small secluded lake in the Sierra National Forest along the San Joaquin River. It rests at about 1,200 feet elevation. Its a very pretty lake with lots of greenery down to the water line. It stays full most of the year and is not subject to severe draw down. The paddle up stream on the San Joaquin River past the PG&E power station is quite beautiful (except for the power station). Motors of any kind are prohibited on Kerckoff Lake. It gets hotter than Hades in the summer here. Be sure to avail yourself of the excellent swimming. Nearby Redinger Lake offers more of a long distance paddling experience in the company of power boats and jet skis.

Camping   Smalley Cove Recreation Area on Kerckoff Lake has 5 sites with piped water, toilets, tables and fireplaces for a fee, no reservations.

Directions   From Hwy 99 in Madera take Hwy 145 east to Hwy 41, take Hwy 41 north about 25 miles to County Road 200 (North Fork Road), go east and north to the junction with Road 222 (Auberry Road) just south of the the town of North Fork, go south on Road 222 for about 6 miles to Kerckoff Lake and Smalley Cove Recreation Area.

Resources   Sierra National Forest map from USFS, Cascade Point topo map from USGS.

Advisory   Due to extreme fire danger in the area most years, campfires are prohibited.

Information   Sierra National Forest : 209-877-2218, Pacific Gas & Electric: 530-386-5164.

Greenery right down to the water at Kerckoff Lake

The San Joaquin River enters Kerckoff Lake

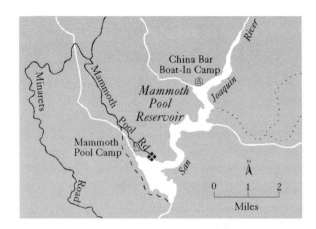

Mammoth Pool Reservoir from the road at 5,000 feet

Chiquito Creek enters Mammoth Pool

Mammoth Pool Reservoir

Description   With all the granite boulders and peaks you would swear you're at a high mountain, alpine lake, but Mammoth Pool Reservoir sits at only 3,300 feet elevation. The walls of the Stanislaus River in which this narrow lake resides, rise more than 2,000 feet up from the shoreline. Mammoth Pool has it all for the canoer: majestic alpine scenery, paddle-in camping and intimate, narrow canyons to explore. On the road in keep an eye out to the northeast for your first eye-popping view of Mammoth Pool Reservoir and the mountains beyond.

Camping   All these campgrounds have tables, fireplaces, and toilets for a fee, no reservations: Placer, 7 sites for tents only, no water - Sweet Water, 10 sites (5 for tents only), no water - Mammoth Pool, 47 sites (18 for tents only), piped water.

Directions   From Hwy 99 in Madera take Hwy 145 east to Hwy 41, take Hwy 41 north about 25 miles to County Road 200 (North Fork Road), go east and north to the town of North Fork, from North Fork go east and south on Road 225 to the junction of Minarets Road, go southeast then north on Minarets Road for about 40 miles to Mammoth Pool Road, go south on Mammoth Pool Road to the campgrounds and lake.

Resources   Sierra National Forest map from USFS, Squaw Dome and Mammoth Pool Dam topo maps from USGS.

Advisory   The reservoir is closed from May 1st - June 16th. Summer thunderstorms can bring rain and lightning. Get off the water during thunderstorms. Watch for power boats. Bring your own.

Information   Sierra National Forest: 209-683-4665

Huntington Lake

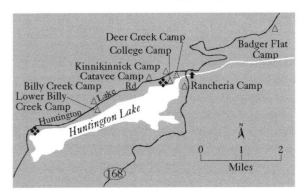

Description   Huntington Lake sits at 7,000 feet elevation among pine forests. The lake is 5 miles long and a half mile wide with 14 miles of shoreline to explore. It's a beautiful, man-made lake with the trees coming right down to the shore all the way around the lake. There's plenty of camping here and it makes good base camp for exploring the rest of the lakes in the area. Summer use is heavy and power boats and jet skis are allowed on Huntington Lake, so avoid the middle of the lake on crowded days.

Camping   All these campgrounds have piped water, tables, fireplaces and toilets for a fee, reservations through 800-280-2267: Billy Creek, 77 sites (57 for tents only), flush toilets - Catavee, 31 sites - Kinnickinick, 35 sites, flush toilets - College, 11 sites - Deer Creek, 28 sites, flush toilets - Rancheria, 150 sites, flush toilets. Badger Flat campground has 15 sites with tables, fireplaces and toilets, but no water for a fee, no reservations.

Looking southwest over Huntington Lake

Directions   From Hwy 99 in Fresno go north on Hwy 168 for 75 miles to the lake and campgrounds.

Resources   Sierra National Forest map from USFS, Kaiser Peak and Huntington Lake topo maps from USGS.

Advisory   Summer thunderstorms can bring rain and lightning. Get off the water during thunderstorms. Watch for power boats.

Information   Sierra National Forest: 209-841-3311, Huntington Lake Resort Marina: 209-893-6750

Huntington Lake's eastern end

The view from Kaiser Pass Road

Tiny, intimate Ward Lake

Granite is everywhere at Florence Lake

Florence & Edison Lakes

Description You want to get way out there? This is way out there. You have to drive on a twisting one lane road over Kaiser Pass (9,170 ft.) just to get there. The drive in has some of the most awesomely beautiful scenery to be seen in California.

Edison Lake sits at 7,650 feet elevation amongst granite peaks that tower over its east end. Edison Lake has a strictly enforced 15 m.p.h. speed limit, allowing paddler's to travel in peace. On the way to Edison Lake, Mono Hot Springs has naturally heated mineral baths. The Pacific Crest Trail is very near the east end of the lake.

Florence Lake sits at 7,327 feet elevation and granite is everywhere, boulders, slabs, shoreline and surrounding mountains. Even the big concrete dam seems part of the powerful image of this gorgeous lake. The day I was there wind and whitecaps had taken over the lake. Even in the wind, the beauty of the place was overwhelming. On the way to Florence Lake you will pass tiny, serene Ward Lake which is well worth a paddle.

Camping Vermillion Campground, 31 sites (11 for tents only) and Jackass Meadow Campground, 44 sites both have tables, fireplaces, toilets and piped water for a fee, reservations through 800-280-2267. Trail Camp boat-in camp, Upper Vermillion boat-in camp and Ward Lake all have a few primitive sites with tables, fireplaces and toilets, but no water, no fee, no reservations.

Directions From Hwy 99 in Fresno go north on Hwy 168 for 75 miles to Huntington Lake, at the east end of Huntington Lake continue on Kaiser Pass Road up (way up) and over the hill (big hill) about 13 miles to the fork in the road, the right fork goes east to Ward and Florence Lakes, the left fork goes north to Mono Hot Springs and Edison Lake. This is a very steep, winding, one lane road. Don't bring a trailer or a long RV on this road. You will get stuck, I saw it happen. Definitely not for sqeemish drivers.

Resources Sierra National Forest map from USFS - Sharkstooth Peak, Graveyard Peak, Mount Givens, Florence Lake and Ward Mountain topo maps from USGS.

Advisory Summer thunderstorms can bring rain and lightning. Get off the water during thunderstorms. Afernoon winds can get quite strong on both lakes. Bring your own water.

Information Sierra National Forest: 209-855-5360, Vermillion Valley Resort (Edison Lake): 209-855-6558, Florence Lake Resort: 209-966-3195

The Vermillion Cliffs behind Lake Edison

A granite wall rises from Ward Lake

Awesome peaks surround Florence Lake

99

Distinctive granite "mounds" surround Courtright Reservoir

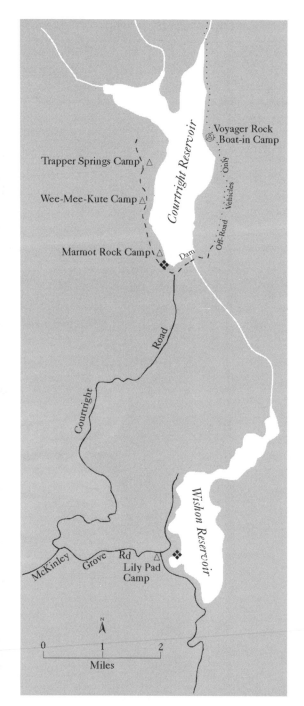

Looking up the NorthFork Kings River gorge at Wishon Reservoir's north end

Courtright & Wishon Reservoirs

Description   Courtright Reservoir sits at 8,170 feet elevation and is surrounded by distinctive granite mounds. I don't know how else to the describe these plentiful granite formations. There very different for a highland feature and quite beautiful. It gives the lake a sort of magical, fantasy atmosphere. The 15 m.p.h speed limit here sends water skiers and jet skis to faster waters, leaving the lake to paddlers and anglers in small boats.

Wishon Reservoir sits on the North Fork Kings River at 6,539 feet elevation. It's a beatiful lake with deep blue water, forested shoreline, mountain peak and pretty little side creeks. It goes from the an open water lake in the south near the dam, through a narrow gorge, and then opens up again at its northern end. Power boats and jet skis are allowed on the lake, but there is a 15 m.p.h. speed limit through the gorge and at the north end of the lake.

Camping   These campgrounds have tables, fireplaces, toilets and piped water for a fee, no reservations: Lily Pad, 16 sites (6 for tents only) - Trapper Springs, 45 sites - Marmot Rock Walk-In, 14 sites for tents only. Voyager Rock Boat-In has some primitive sites with fireplaces and toilets for free, no reservations. You can drive to Voyager campground, but only with 4-wheel-drive.

Directions   From Hwy 99 in Fresno go north on Hwy 168 for 63 miles to the town of Shaver Lake, from Shaver Lake go east on Dinky Creek Road about 12 miles, follow the sign for Courtright & Wishon Reservoirs and go further east on McKinley Grove Road about 14 miles to a fork in the road, again follow the signs, the left fork goes 10 miles to Courtright Reservoir, the right fork goes 3 miles to Wishon Reservoir.

Resources   Sierra National Forest map from USFS - Ward Mountaian, Courtright Reservoir and Rough Spur topo maps from USGS.

Advisory   Watch for power boats on south Wishon. Summer thunderstorms can bring rain and lightning. Get off the water during thunderstorms.

Information   Sierra National Forest : 209-855-8321, Pacific Gas & Electric: 800-743-5000.

Wishon Reservoir's more open southern end

Storm clouds brew over Courtright Reservoir

Short Hair Creek enters Wishon Reservoir

101

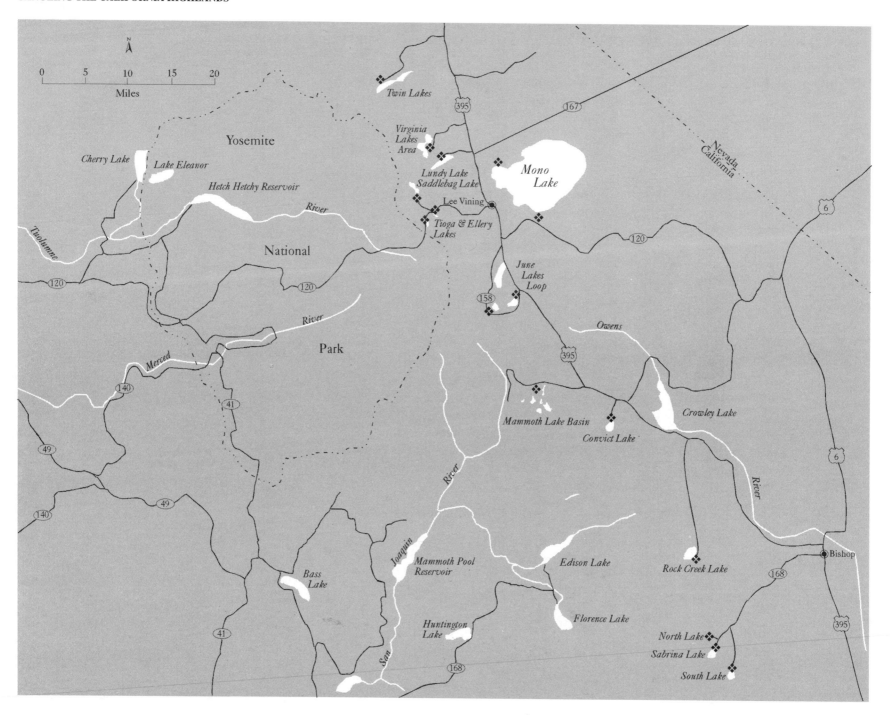

The High Sierra

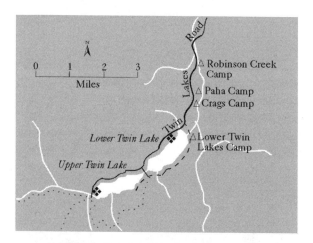

Twin Lakes

Description
Twin Lakes sits at 7000 ft. elevation and is actually two separate lakes with very distinct personalities. Upper Twin Lake is surrounded by granite peaks and is the prettier of the two lakes. Upper Twin allows power boats, water skiing and jet skiing. Lower Twin Lake has a 5 m.p.h. speed limit, so you don't have to watch out for big wakes. Lower Twin also has a nice creek paddle at its west end up Robinson Creek that makes for an intimate exploration. Open May through October.

Camping
These campgrounds all have tables, fireplaces and piped water for a fee. Reserve through at 800-280-CAMP. Flush toilets and showers are available nearby. Lower Twin Lake (15 sites), Crags (27 sites), Paha (22 sites), Robinson Creek (54 sites).

Directions
From the town of Bridgeport go south on Twin Lake Road to the lakes, campgrounds and boat ramps.

Resources
Toiyabe National Forest map from USFS, Twin Lakes topo map from USGS.

Advisory
Watch for power boats on Upper Twin Lake. Winds can get quite strong in the afternoon. Early fall through late spring snows can make this area inaccessible. Closed in winter.

Information
Bridgeport Ranger District/Toiyabe National Forest: 619-932-7070.

Granite peaks surround Upper Twim Lake

Robinson Creek off the west end of Lower Twin Lake

Virginia Lakes Area

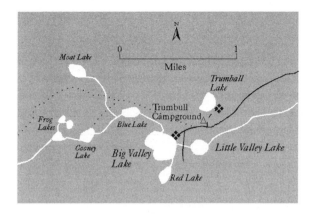

Description This beautiful high mountain area sits at 9,700 feet elevation. There are 15 small, natural lakes in the area, 3 of which are accessible by car: Trumbull Lake, Little Valley Lake and Big Valley Lake. Trumbull Lake is a natural lake - perfect for a quiet float. It is small, surrounded by lush green grasses, and has an almost mystical feel about it. Big Valley Lake is the largest of the three and is more of a paddle than a float. It has two waterfalls entering into it - an exquisite little one at its southeast corner and a big one at its north end. If you're careful, you can hike to the top of the northern waterfall for a great view of Big Valley Lake. Gas motors are prohibited on all these lakes and there is a 10 m.p.h. speed limit, so you won't have to worry about power boat wakes.

With an inflatable kayak that can be carried in a pack you can easily hike a few miles into the Hoover Wilderness and float on some lakes that rarely see a boat. The historic ghost town of Bodie is nearby. Horseback trips into the back country are also available. The Virginia Lakes area is open June through October.

Camping Trumbull Lake campground has 45 campsites with water, toilets, tables and fireplaces for a fee. Reservations can be made through Destinet (1-800-283-CAMP). For those who wish a more pampered stay, Virginia Lake Resort (619-647-6484) has cabins and full amenities.

Directions From Hwy 395 south of Bridgeport and north of Lee Vining go west on Virginia Lake Road to Trumbull campground and the lakes.

Resources Toiyabe National Forest map from USFS, Dunderberg Peak topo map from USGS.

Advisory Early fall through late spring snows can make this area inaccessible. Closed in winter.

Information Bridgeport Ranger District: 619-932-7070.

Deep, cold, clear water of Big Valley Lake

105

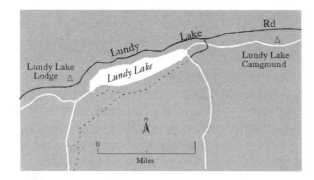

Sea gull a long way from the ocean

Majestic mountains around Lundy Lake

Lundy Lake

Description
Lundy Lake sits at 7,900 feet elevation in the Lundy Canyon fed by Mill Creek. At one mile long and a half a mile wide, you can definitely get in some paddle strokes on this long lake. Pine and aspen trees cover the canyon's granite walls. The lake is surrounded by some magnificent mountains: Mount Olson, Mount Scowden, and Glacier Peak. The lake is open from June through October.
A trailhead takes off from the east end of the lake and runs along Mill Creek into the 20 Lakes Basin of Hoover Wilderness Area to Saddlebag Lake. There are several waterfalls and beaver ponds along the way (make sure you have a shuttle back to your car at Lundy Lake).

Camping
Mill Creek campground, run by Mono County Parks, has 54 campsites with toilets, tables and fireplaces, for a fee, no reservations. Lundy Lake Resort offers 27 tent sites and three camp huts with full amenities, for a fee.

Directions
From Hwy 395, at the junction of Hwy 167, go west on Lundy Lake Road to the lake and campgrounds.

Resources
Inyo National Forest map from USFS, Lundy topo map from USGS.

Advisory
Early fall through late spring snows can make this area inaccessible. Closed in winter.

Information
Mono County Parks, 619-932-7911. Lundy Lake Resort, P.O.Box 265, Lee Vining, CA 93541

Mono Lake

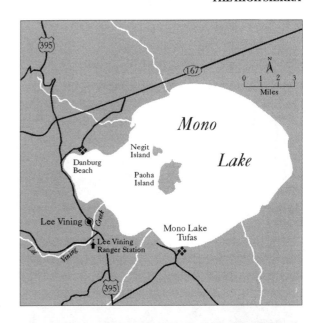

Description   Mono Lake is the last remnant of an ancient inland sea and sits in the high desert at 7,200 feet elevation. This huge lake is 13 miles east to west and 8 miles north to south. The water is three times more salty and eighty times more alkaline than sea water. The lake is fed by five streams and numerous underground springs. It has no outlet other than evaporation. The lake gets its name from the Yokuts Indian word "Mono" which stands for the "brine flies" which blacken the shoreline.

Man's impact on this area can be most definitively seen here at Mono Lake. In 1941 Los Angeles started draining the waters that feed Mono Lake. The lake level lowered, exposing odd tufa formations. Made of hard calcium carbonate, the tufa rose up as mineral springs bubbled up from the bottom of the lake bed. They give the lake a very alien feel, sort of like an ocean on the moon. The most prolific example of the tufas is on the south shore of the lake at South Tufa. Paddling among the tufas or out to the islands are the main canoeing attractions of Mono Lake. In 1995 an agreement was reached between the state and the city of Los Angeles to stop the diverting of Mono Lakes feed water, and the lake will be allowed to return to its natural level in the next few decades.

Mono Lake is a major stopover along the Pacific Flyway. Ninety-five percent of *all* California gulls nest at Mono Lake on Negit and Pahoa Islands. Abundant brine shrimp and flies fill the lake and its shore, feeding the gulls.

Camping   Lee Vining Creek Campgrounds, Big Bend Campground, and Aspen Grove Campground have water, tables, fire-rings and toilets for a fee, no reservations.

Directions   Right next to Hwy 395, at the junction with Hwy 120 and the town of Lee Vining. You literally can't miss it.

Resources   Inyo National Forest map from USFS - Lundy, Negit Island, Sulphur Pond, Mount Dana, Lee Vining and Mono Mills topo maps from USGS - brochure from the California Department of Parks and Recreation.

Advisory   Afternoon winds can be dangerously fierce if you get caught out in the middle of this huge lake. From April 1 to August 1 stay a mile from Negit & Paoha Islands to protect the nesting gulls. Wash the mineral water off your canoe, or it will stain.

Information   California Department of Parks and Recreation, 619-647-6331.

The majestic peaks of the Sierra Nevada loom above Mono Lake

Close encounters of the tufa kind

107

Looking north across Saddlebag Lake

The highest lake you can reach by car in California

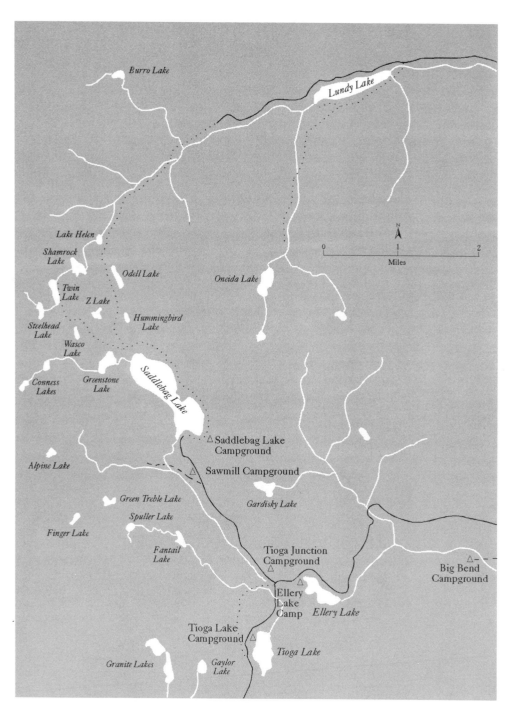

Saddlebag, Tioga & Ellery Lakes

Description   At 10,087 feet elevation, Saddlebag Lake is the highest lake in California accessible by car. The lake is surrounded by majestic mountain peaks. Only fishing boats are allowed on the lake, no water-skiing. A trailhead to the 20 Lakes Basin of the Hoover Wilderness area takes off from the lake. You can hike all the way to Lundy Lake (make sure you have a shuttle back to your car at Saddlebag Lake). The lake is open June through October.

Tioga and Ellery Lakes are two pristine alpine lakes that rest at the crest of Tioga Pass in the Sierra Nevada at 9,600 feet elevation. Being right next to Hwy 120 makes the lakes readily accessible. Only small fishing motors are allowed on the water, so big power boat wakes are not a problem. Yosemite National Park, Tuolumne Meadows, and the ghost town of Bennettville are nearby. The lakes are open June through October.

Camping   Saddlebag Campground has 22 sites with water, flush toilets, tables and fireplaces for a fee, no reservations. Junction Campground has 10 campsites with toilets, tables and fireplaces, no fee, no reservations. Sawmill Campground has 12 walk-in campsites, no fee, no reservations. Tioga Lake Campground has 13 tent sites with flush toilets, water, tables and fireplaces for a fee, no reservations. Ellery Lake Campground has 13 campsites, including 3 for tents only with water, flush toilets, tables and fireplaces for a fee, no reservations.

Directions   Just south of the town of Lee Vining on Hwy 395, take Hwy 120 west toward Yosemite National Park. Tioga and Ellery Lakes are on the south side of the highway. The turnoff for Saddlebag Lake is also off Hwy 120, between Tioga and Ellery Lakes, turn north on Saddlebag Road to the campground and lake.

Resources   Inyo National Forest map from USFS, Tioga Pass and Mount Dana topo map from USGS.

Advisory   Early fall through late spring snows can make this area inaccessible. Hwy 120 is closed in winter. The road into Saddlebag lake is steep and winding - trailers and RVs are not advised.

Information   Mono Lake Ranger District: 619-647-6525.

Tioga Lake at the eastern gateway to Yosemite

The road between Ellery Lake & Saddlebag Lake

Ellery Lake is golden in the evening light

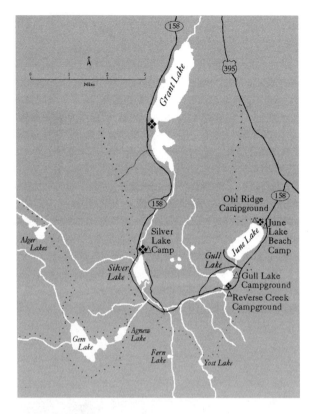

Silver Lake

June Lakes Loop

Description These four alpine lakes that make up the June Lake Loop sit at 7,600 feet elevation and are interconnected by streams and creeks: June Lake (160 acres), Gull Lake (64 acres), Silver Lake (80 acres) and Grant Lake (1000 acres). June, Gull & Silver have a 10 m.p.h. speed limit on all boats with motors. The trailhead into Ansel Adams Wilderness Area heads off from the Rush Creek Trailhead campground at Silver Lake.

Camping June Lake campground has 22 campsites with water, tables, flush toilets and fireplaces for a fee, no reservations. Oh! Ridge Campground on June Lake has 148 campsites with water, flush toilets, tables, fireplaces and a laundromat for a fee, reserve through 800-283-CAMP. Gull Lake Campground has 11 campsites with water, flush toilets, tables and fireplaces for a fee, no reservations; Rush Creek Trailhead next to Silver Lake Campground has water, toilets, tables and fireplaces for a fee, no reservations. There are also many rental cabins in the area call the June Lake Chamber of Commerce for information,

Directions From Hwy 395 south of the town of Lee Vining, take Hwy 158 which is the June Lakes Loop and passes by all of the lakes.

Resources Inyo National Forest map from USFS, June Lake topo map from USGS.

Advisory Watch for power boats on Grant Lake. Early fall through late spring snows can make this area inaccessible. Closed in winter.

Information Mono Lake Ranger District, 619-647-6525. June Lake Chamber of Commerce, 619-648-7584

Mammoth Lakes Basin

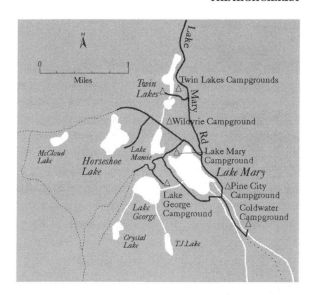

Description The Mammoth Lakes Basin has 9 exquisitely beautiful, snowmelt filled, glacier-carved lakes at an elevation of 8,500 to 9,250 feet. Nearby John Muir Wilderness and Ansel Adams Wilderness are well worth exploring if you have the time and a good pair of hiking boots. Devil's Postpile National Monument and Rainbow Falls are also nearby. During the winter this area is kept open for cross-country skiing.

Camping All of the campgrounds in the area have water, flush toilets, tables, fireplaces and a laundromat for a fee with no reservations: Twin Lakes Campground (94 campsites, 23 for tents only), Lake George Campground (16 campsites), Lake Mary Campground (48 campsites), Pine City Campground (11 campsites), and Coldwater Campground (77 campsites). There are also many rental cabins in the area. Call the Mammoth Lakes Visitor's Center for information.

Directions From Hwy 395 south of Lee Vining take Hwy 203 west to Lake Mary Road. Go south on Lake Mary Road to the lakes and campgrounds.

Resources Inyo National Forest map from USFS, Crystal Crag topo map from USGS.

Advisory Early fall through late spring snows can make this area inaccessible.

Information Mammoth Lakes Visitors Center, 619-924-5000.

High Sierra Lakes are ideal for family canoeing

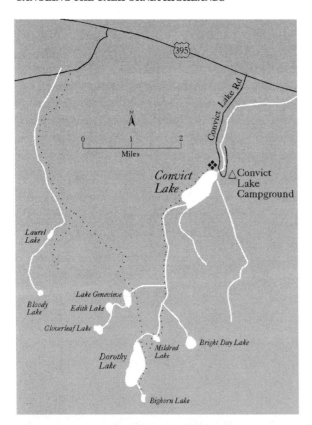

Convict Lake

Description   Convict Lake rests in a bowl of granite peaks at 7,583 feet elevation with 3 miles of shoreline to explore. Fed by snowmelt from mountain peaks surrounding the lake, the water is cold and clear. There is a 10 m.p.h. speed limit making it ideal for canoeists. The lake borders right on the John Muir Wilderness with several pristine alpine lakes within a day's hike. There are horseback riding facilities available. Open April through October.

Camping   Convict Lake Campground has 88 sites with water, tables, fireplaces and flush toilets for a fee; no reservations. There are also rustic cabin facilities at the Convict Lake Resort.

Directions   South of Mammoth Lakes on Hwy 395 turn south on Convict Lake Road to the lake and campground.

Resources   Inyo National Forest map from USFS, Convict Lake and Bloody Mountain topo maps from USGS.

Advisory   Early fall through late spring snows can make this area inaccessible. Closed in winter.

Information   Inyo National Forest, 619-924-5500

Crystal clear waters of Convict Lake

Rock Creek Lake

Description   Rock Creek lake is a granite-bound lake on the eastern slope of the Sierra. This little 63 acre lake rest at 9,680 feet in the Little Lakes Valley on Rock Creek Canyon. Motor boats are not a problem here since there is a 5 m.p.h. speed limit. There are many hiking trails to explore in this beautiful area that is adjacent to the John Muir Wilderness.

Camping   Rock Creek Lake campground has 28 campsites with water, flush toilets, tables, fireplaces and a laundromat for a fee, no reservations.

Directions   From Hwy 395 between Lee Vining and Bishop take Rock Creek Road south to the lake and campground.

Resources   Inyo National Forest from USFS, Mount Morgan topo map from USGS.

Advisory   Early fall through late spring snows can make this area inaccessible. Closed in winter.

Information   White Mountain Ranger District, 619-873-4207.

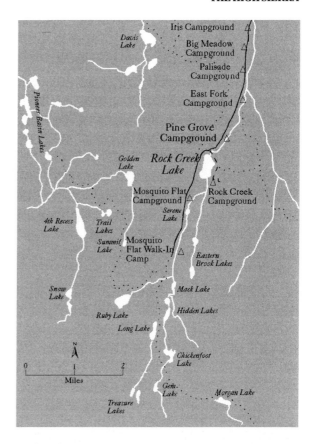

Rock Creek Lake lies intimately nestled among mountain peaks

Lake Sabrina sits in its granite bowl

Tiny, quiet North Lake

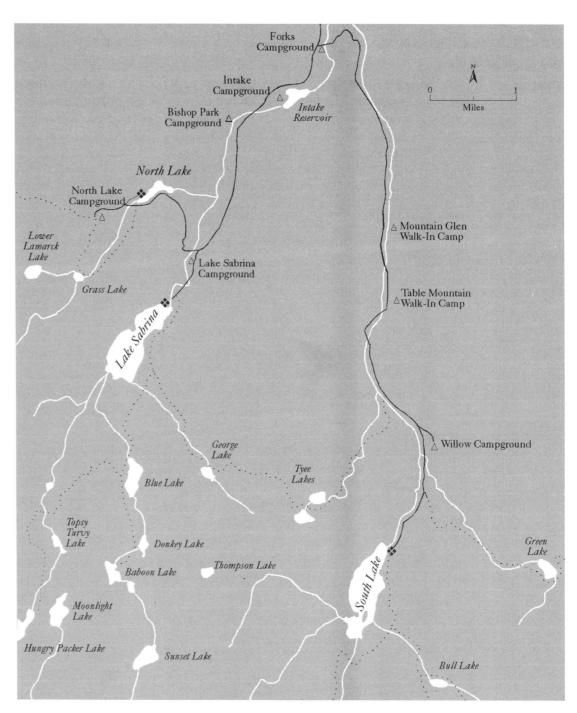

Sabrina, North & South Lakes

Description Lake Sabrina (150 acres), South Lake (180 acres) and tiny North Lake are nestled among steep granite walls at 7,500-9,500 feet elevation along Bishop Creek. The scenery is breathtaking and the water is clear and cold. The is a 5 m.p.h. on these three lakes making them ideal for canoeing. These lakes sit right on the boundary of the John Muir Wilderness Area and next to Kings Canyon National Park, providing ample hiking opportunities.

Camping All of these campgrounds have water, flush toilets, tables, fireplaces and a laundromat for a fee, no reservations: Sabrina (18 campsites), Forks (8 campsites), Big Trees (9 campsites), Bishop Park (21 campsites), Intake (17 campsites), Four Jeffrey (106 campsites). North Lake campground has 11 sites for tent only with water, toilets, tables and fireplaces for a fee, no reservations.

Directions From Hwy 395 in Bishop take Hwy 168 south to the campgrounds, Lake Sabrina, and North Lake. For South Lake turn off Hwy 168 onto South Lake Road.

Resources Inyo National Forest map from USFS, Mount Darwin and Mount Thompson topo maps from USGS.

Advisory Early fall through late spring snows can make this area inaccessible. Closed in winter.

Information USFS in Bishop: 619-873-4207 or the White Mountain Ranger District: 619-873-2500.

Glaciated granite peaks above South Lake

Sunlight at play on South Lake

Canoe Manned by Voyageurs Passing a Waterfall, Francis Ann Hopkins, 1869

National Archives of Canada, C-002771

Suggested Reading

Canoeing

Canoeing A Trailside Guide ~ by Gordon Grant: A great color book on canoeing basics: choosing a canoe and paddle, canoe design, tandem and solo paddle strokes...very thorough with beautiful photographs and clear illustrations.

Outdoor Pursuits Series: Canoeing ~ by Laurie Gullion: Another great color book on the basics of canoeing with an outstanding section on warm up exercises for paddling. There is a bonus section on some world wide paddling destination.

Path Of The Paddle~by Bill Mason: Bill Mason was the Grandfather of all paddlers. This book on basic canoeing skills is a classic.

Song Of The Paddle ~ by Bill Mason: Bill Mason's book on canoe camping. Bill was the quintessential outdoorsman and his witty writing style make this book a pleasure to read.

The Essentials Of Solo Canoeing ~ by Cliff Jacobson: A nice little book on going it alone in a canoe. Bring it along on a trip for a little light reading. Paddling alone has its own rewards.

Maps

National Forest Maps ~ Published by the United States Forest Service (USFS): Indispensible resource! These maps have the most current information of any maps available, especially road type (paved, dirt, gravel, 4 wheel drive, trails, etc.). I would suggest getting all the National Forest maps listed in this book. They're very useful and they're fun to play with. They are available through the U.S. Forest Service, 630 Sansome St., San Francisco, CA 94111: 415-705-2874.

US Geological Survey Maps ~ Published by the United States Geological Survey (USGS): These are the most detailed maps you can get of any area. They show everything, although, some are a little out of date on new roads and housing developments. You can get an index of California's topographical maps by calling the USGS Branch Of Distribution in Denver, Colorado at 303-236-7477.

Northern California Atlas & Gazetter ~ Published by Del Lorme Mapping Company: Great resource! Topographical maps covering all of Northern California from just south of San Francisco to the Oregon border.

Southern California Atlas & Gazetter ~ Published by Del Lorme Mapping Company: Topographical maps covering all of Southern California from just south of San Francisco to the Mexico border.

Camping

California Camping~By Tom Stienstra: Awesome resource! This book is a must for the California camper. Lists virtually every campground in California. I never go outdoors overnight without it. Priceless resource for planning your paddling explorations.

Camper's Companion~By Rick Greensan & Hal Kahn: This book is filled with lots of good advise on camping. You want to be prepared and comfortable when you camp out. This book will get you there.

Periodicals

Canoe & Kayak: A national publication that features paddling issues. They cover everything: regional and world-wide destinations, water-oriented enviromental issues, paddle gear, reviews of book and gear, quiet water, white water and sea water.

Paddler: Another national paddling publications. Also covers a wide range of paddling issues. Very informative and entertaining.

Sea Kayaker: Obviously, the focus here is on the paddling the ocean, but once you become a fanatic paddler, you'll want to get into it all.

California Natural History

A Natural History of California ~ by Allan A. Schoenherr: This book covers everything about the natural world of California: basic ecology and geology, climate, rocks, plants and animals. Broken down into ecological regions, this book really does justice to the natural diversity of California.

Index of Lakes

Name	Page	Natural Lake	Paddle-In Camping	Lakeside Camping	Winter Access	Long Distance Paddling	No Motors/ Speed Limits	Exquisite Beauty
Emerald Lake	22	*					*	*
Englebright Reservoir	56		*	*	*	*		
Fall River Valley	38	*	*	*	*	*	*	*
Fallen Leaf Lake	79	*		*		*		*
Faucherie Lake	60		*	*			*	*
Feeley Lake	60		*	*			*	*
Florence Lake	98			*			*	*
Frenchman Reservoir	51			*		*		
French Meadows Reservoir	68		*	*		*		*
Fuller Lake	60			*			*	*
Gerle Creek Reservoir	76						*	*
Grant Lake	110							
Grouse Ridge Area	60			*			*	*
Hell Hole Reservoir	69		*	*		*		*
Highland Lakes	90	*					*	*
Horseshoe Lake	111						*	
Huntington Lake	97			*		*		
Ice House Reservoir	73			*				
Ice Lakes	71	*		*		*		
Indian Creek Reservoir	82			*			*	*
Iron Gate Reservoir	12			*	*	*		
Jackson Meadow Reservoir	62		*	*		*		*
June Lake	110	*		*				*
June Lakes Loop	110	*		*				*
Juniper Lake	22	*					*	*
Kangaroo Lake	13	*					*	*
Kelly Lake	70	*		*			*	
Kerckoff Lake	95			*	*		*	
Kidd Lake	71						*	*
Kinney Reservoir	90						*	*
Kirkwood Lake	84	*					*	*
Lake Almanor	28			*		*		
Lake Alpine	88			*			*	*

Name	Page	Natural Lake	Paddle-In Camping	Lakeside Camping	Winter Access	Long Distance Paddling	No Motors/ Speed Limits	Exquisite Beauty
Lake Britton	36			*	*	*		
Lake Clementine	67		*	*	*	*		*
Lake Davis	50			*		*		
Lake George	111						*	*
Lake Helen	22						*	*
Lake Juanita	14						*	
Lake Mamie	111						*	*
Lake Mary	111			*			*	*
Lake McCloud	17				*	*		
Lake Sabrina	114						*	*
Lake Siskiyou	16				*		*	*
Lake Tahoe	80	*	*	*		*		*
Lake Valley Reservoir	70			*		*	*	
Lake Van Norden	71						*	*
Lakes Basin	54	*		*			*	*
Lewiston Lake	18			*	*	*	*	*
Lily Lake	35	*					*	*
Little Valley Lake	105	*					*	*
Long Lake	26	*					*	
Loon Lake	76		*	*		*		*
Lindsey Lake	60						*	*
Little Grass Valley Reservoir	53			*				
Lower Blue Lake	86			*			*	*
Lower Bucks Lake	48			*			*	
Lundy Lake	106			*			*	*
Mammoth Lakes Basin	111			*			*	*
Mammoth Pool Reservoir	96		*	*		*		*
Manzanita Lake (Cascade)	22	*					*	
Manzanita Lake (Southwest)	94	*			*		*	*
McMurray Lake	60						*	*
Medicine Lake	15	*		*				
Milton Reservoir	62			*			*	*
Mono Lake	107	*				*	*	*

Name	Page	Natural Lake	Paddle-In Camping	Lakeside Camping	Winter Access	Long Distance Paddling	No Motors/ Speed Limits	Exquisite Beauty
Mountain Meadow Reservoir	29					*		
North Battle Creek Reservoir	21			*			*	
North Lake	114	*					*	*
Red Lake	84			*			*	*
Redinger Lake	95			*	*	*		
Rock Creek Lake	113						*	*
Round Valley Reservoir	46			*			*	
Saddlebag Lake	108					*	*	*
Salt Springs Reservoir	83					*	*	*
Sawmill Lake	60		*	*			*	*
Silver Lake (High Sierra)	110	*		*			*	*
Silver Lake (Cascade)	24	*		*			*	*
Silver Lake (North Sierra)	48	*					*	*
Silver Lake (Tahoe Sierra)	84	*		*		*		*
Sly Creek Reservoir	52			*	*	*	*	
Smith Lake	48	*		*			*	
Snake Lake	48	*		*			*	*
South Lake	114						*	*
Spicer Meadow Reservoir	88					*	*	*
Stumpy Meadows Reservoir	72			*			*	
Sugar Pine Reservoir	66			*	*		*	*
Summit Lake	22	*		*			*	*
Tamarack Lake	86			*			*	*
Tioga Lake	108			*			*	*
Trinity Lake	18		*	*	*	*		
Truckee River & Marsh	80	*				*	*	*
Trumball Lake	105	*		*			*	*
Tule Lake	32						*	
Twin Lake(Tahoe Sierra)	86						*	
Twin Lakes (High Sierra)	104			*			*	*
Twin Lakes (Mammoth Lakes)	111			*			*	*
Union Reservoir	88			*			*	*
Union Valley Reservoir	74			*				

Name	Page	Natural Lake	Paddle-In Camping	Lakeside Camping	Winter Access	Long Distance Paddling	No Motors/ Speed Limits	Exquisite Beauty
Upper Blue Lake	86			*			*	*
Utica Reservoir	88		*	*			*	*
Virginia Lakes Area	105	*					*	*
Weaver Lake	60						*	*
Whiskeytown Reservoir	20			*	*	*		
Wilson Lake	27	*		*			*	
Wishon Reservoir	100		*	*		*	*	*
Woods Lake	84	*		*			*	*
Wrights Lake	75						*	*

The author doing what he likes best, paddling on a lake

John Coale was born in 1954 in San Francisco and has spent all of his life living and traveling in California. Since 1991 John has spent his spare time seeking out the canoeable waters of California. This book is the first of his books on quiet water canoeing destinations, with more to follow. John has a daughter named Taiowa and a cat named Dinkers. He has been a chimney sweep for 15 years. When John is not working or canoeing he's playing music on a plethora of different instruments. He's been a musician for 27 years. "Playing music and playing in nature is what sets my spirit free and heals my wounds."

Remember what Johnny sez:

"It's all right to have a good time!"

What are you still doing here?
Go get your paddle wet!

Notes

Notes

Notes